GW01316196

Jo

Jo Hawkins

DEDICATION

I want to dedicate this 'Life Story' to my family, all 17 of them!

Next, I want to dedicate it to my beloved husband Phil, who has not only encouraged and supported me in writing the book, but more importantly – he has been my loving companion and support throughout our life together, with all its challenges and joys.

Lastly and most importantly, I wish to acknowledge the faithfulness of my beloved Lord Jesus from before my birth until the end of my life and beyond.

.

Jo Hawkins – July 2013

CONTENTS

ACKNOWLEDGMENTS

I want to thank my daughter Vicki, for all the time and skill and many hours she has spent in bringing about the publishing of this 'Life Story.' Also the feedback and helpful comments from my husband Phil, and friends and family who have read the earlier drafts.

1 EARLY MEMORIES

"Not another girl!"

These inspiring words greeted my emergence into the world on Sunday February 8 1931. Whether the doctor was a confirmed male chauvinist, or whether he just felt sorry for my mother I will never know. However, thankfully my mother did not share his sentiments! I never had any reason to feel I was an unwanted intrusion into my parents and older sister's life, even though it was nearly 6 years since Rosemary arrived on the Thorneloe scene.

How sad that she, an intelligent dark haired little 6 year old, was not allowed to follow the progress of my development in her mother's ever increasing "tummy" - and experience the thrill of feeling my little feet kicking against her hand. In those days in our house, it was not "done" to talk about such "rude" things as sex and babies in wombs. The first Romie knew (later to become my pet name for her) of my imminent arrival were the rows of "dolls" clothes hanging on the ancient hot-water cylinder in the bathroom! Her Nanny, Mimmy, informed her that if she was a very good girl, she would have a new little baby brother or sister to play with soon ' I shudder to imagine my fate if she had failed to rise to that lofty standard!

1

My earliest memories of my parents Edward and Phyllis Thorneloe are scattered and mostly positive. I still recall the long walks riding on my father's shoulders down Barby Lane out into the country passed the famous Rugby School, and the times he took me to see the trains at the large Rugby Junction. I recall with pleasure the many occasions we stood on the platform as the huge express trains approached pulled by such engines as the Coronation Scot and the Royal Scot, my small heart beating rapidly with excitement as the train thundered through belching steam and sparks. We often got a friendly wave from the coal smeared and "heroic" driver! Father would often talk to me as I rode aloft, and one day I remember him explaining how sound takes time to travel by showing me a factory chimney in the distance where smoke spurted out at intervals and a bang-reached our ears a few seconds later. He was good at explaining things and had a wide general knowledge of everyday facts.

The reason we often went on walks without mother was that she was serving in our shop, which sold women's clothes. We lived above the shop in a building that was over 500 years old. The business was dependent on mother, and customers came again and again because of her. She was interested in people and a very good saleswoman. Before mother married my father, she had been to Homerton College, Cambridge, to train to be a teacher. She then taught for a few years in Lincolnshire in conditions which modern teachers would find amazing! This was 1916 and a class could be as large as ninety pupils! - they ranged from five to fourteen years. Amongst the tales mother told was that of the bargees' children who dropped in when their parents' barge was tied up at the local wharf. She looked up from her desk one day to see an eye staring at her from the top of the front desk! It was the glass eye of the poor child who found it too painful wearing it all the time!! Another child with head bent diligently over her work caused mother to stare in amazement as the hair quivered with the presence of hundreds of head-lice!

Mother was five foot one tall and some of her older boys were over six-foot. One day near the beginning of her career a great strapping lad gave her a bit of cheek, no doubt testing out the diminutive new teacher to see how much he could get away with! So Miss Overton, as she then was, called

him out, bent him over and caned him. From that day on she never had any discipline problems! Years later she met him again, a smart handsome business man and he laughingly reminded her of the caning, much to her embarrassment, blushes and amusement!

By the time mother was engaged to father she was a Deputy Headmistress and, but for the law that married women had to leave teaching, she might well have gone far in the teaching profession. She was a born teacher and could hold a class of children rapt by her personality and dramatic presentation. (I sampled this to a small extent when I was in her Sunday School class - years later).

Because of my mother's involvement in the business, I did not see as much of her as I really needed, and Mimmy our nanny looked after me some of the time. Then one day when I had just turned three years old, a friend mentioned to mother that a new nursery/primary school called Northlands had just opened about a mile from our home. It was an experimental State School and was wonderfully equipped with all the latest Montessori type equipment. It had facilities for children of 3 - 5 years to stay all day, camp beds were provided for an afternoon nap. Every child had their own picture on their pillow, blanket, towel, toothbrush etc. for them to keep for the two years. There was a sandpit and lovely gardens and many toys games and musical instruments and learning equipment. My mother at first was very reluctant to part with me but when she saw the set up she realised that it was ideal for the child of full time working parents (in those days - few mothers went to work).

2 EARLY SCHOOL DAYS

That first day at Northlands is still a vivid memory. The huge room, the amazing toys, the rocking horse, my own things all marked with a picture of a cottage loaf! And dear Miss Roberts - a warm cuddly woman who took me on her knee and immediately made me feel secure and loved. I managed to forgive her for always call me Jozey! It was winter and a huge coal fire was burning in the fireplace by Miss Roberts table, it all seemed so friendly and welcoming. Memories of those early nursery school days still come back to me with pleasure, like the sleeps on our little beds in the afternoon while Miss Roberts softly played Mozart to us, and the time when we put on a concert for our parents. I had to conduct the band, and most of all the quietly controlled and loving atmosphere created by Miss Roberts.

It did me good to be with other children at school, there were so few children where we lived, in the centre of Rugby, and they were mostly boys, so I had grown to like playing boys games - climbing trees and buildings and getting dirty. I might add that I actually looked very much a girl with tight blonde curls and big brown eyes, and some kids asked me if I was Shirley Temple - an illusion which I encouraged with some 'white' and not so white lies. I hated the restrictions of dresses and several times came home with rips in best dresses which mother had taken hours to make.

One Christmas I was bitterly disappointed to wake up and find a baby doll in my stocking. Mother had got a friend to make a beautiful set of

5

clothes for it! I tried not to let mother see how disappointed I was after all the trouble she had been to, but dolls never did anything for me! One of the ways my friends and I spent time, was to go and watch the blacksmith in the lane behind our shop, shoeing horses. That pungent smell as those red-hot shoes met the horse's hooves, still occasionally comes back to me. The blacksmith was a friendly man and he didn't seem to mind us grubby little urchins crowding round the smithy to watch him work with the constant stream of working horses of those days.

JOSE

Another escapade comes to mind that occurred when my cousin John came to stay. By now, I was about nine years old and he was eight. In our back yard was a tiny bit of soil in which grew a massive tree. It must have been 40 feet tall, and its upper branches reached across nearly to our roof. The building was three stories high and the tree had some wonderfully tempting lower branches for climbing. I had never been right to the top, but on this particular day with my cousin John for a playmate, I thought it would be a good opportunity to show off my climbing prowess!! I dared him to climb to the top with me (he told me much later how scared he was but how he did not want to be outdone by a girl!). Up we went, and soon we were level with the roof, it was only a short leap away. I jumped! He jumped and then we had to negotiate the ups and downs of several steep roofs until we came to my attic bedroom window. (The roof outside my bedroom was a glass skylight 3 floors up, one false move! - we would have plunged straight down to the shop floor below). As we came down the stairs to go outside to the back yard again, my mother, who was serving a customer, spotted us and said, "I thought you were both outside, how did you get in here?" Then it all came out, and I was forbidden to ever do such a dangerous thing again!

By now I had left the nursery years far behind and was steadily working my way up the infants classes. I had a "gang" of my own and we wielded a fair bit of power in the playground! I quickly adopted a raw Rugby accent after some kids said - "You talk posh" - never again! My poor mother couldn't understand what had happened to her dear little girl's accent, neither could she understand why I had no voice left at the end of the day until one day she came to fetch me early, and heard me bossing my gang about in the playground! My favourite teacher was young and pretty Miss Perry, she brought out the best in us all. The real shock came when I moved up to the junior part of Northlands and found that not everyone thought the 'sun shone out of me'. In fact my first junior teacher obviously disliked me and in many ways, I don't blame her. I was a bossy little bighead and devious on occasions too! One day we had just gone to the school hall for 'music and movement' when I realised that I had forgotten my pumps. Instead of admitting my mistake, I made up a story about needing to go to the toilet (which I did to salve my conscience) and on the way back I fetched my pumps from the cloakroom. My teacher saw me as I came back and confronted me, she then said something that I have never forgotten! "Go and write out 100 times, I must not be a sneak." Even though I deserved it, writing those words hurt me so much they are carved on my brain!

I was bright and intelligent and was always first or second in the end of term exams at school. I enjoyed life, I had a secure loving home and above all I was confident that God loved me. My mother helped me to know Jesus as a real and intimate friend. When she talked about him her eyes lit up and gradually Jesus became my friend as well as hers. Because my mother had a personal relationship with Jesus, the effect of belonging to the small religious sect called Christadelphians was mainly positive. We read the Bible daily, the Old Testament once, and the New Testament twice in a year. We had a fairly high standard of lay preaching and Bible study classes, all of which laid a good foundation for my life. I was a zealous evangelist at school and loved talking to my friends about my faith. I often arrived home from school with a string of friends, (always the poorest and scruffiest in the class). They hid behind our yard gate while I asked mummy if they could stay for tea! She invariably said yes, and we had a great time. Sometimes in the back yard, we rigged up a Red Indian Camp with a clothes horse and blanket, we dressed up and had war dances, and then for an extra thrill I would take them down into our dark and smelly cellar under the shop. With only one dim light, there were many dark corners and I took great delight in hiding behind a life sized Polar bear (which had advertised Bear Brand stockings in its working life!). Then I would terrify my friends by growling loudly, as they suddenly became aware of the white monster in the dark recesses of the cellar. My parents used to wonder what caused them to rush out of the cellar looking so scared.

On Wednesdays, the shop was closed in the afternoon, and my parents often went to Birmingham to buy more goods for the shop. This gave me a wonderful opportunity to play real shops with my friends, with real counters, real dresses coats and hats and underwear and a marvellous long counter to race around at top speed on the polished floor! The dresses had all been covered with cloths and pushed up one end so that there was ample space to swing on the rails and somersault over them. The 'piece de resistance' was the wedding dress department upstairs! The gorgeous dresses were in an unlocked glass case to protect them from dust, but not from me and my friends - we had a ball! I don't remember us doing any serious damage fortunately!

I had one particular friend called Aileen Gibbs, one day we went for a picnic with our bikes. It was a lovely sunny day and we sat on the bank of a canal to eat our food, then we got the idea of balancing along a girder that stuck out across the canal. I was just in front of Aileen and when she slipped she grabbed hold of me and I fell in! I can still remember the horrible feeling of sinking down and down in the slimy water and the awful fear of drowning. It was just as well that I had learnt to swim a few months before, or I would probably have panicked and drowned. I struggled out of the water, soaking wet, and sat shivering on the grass. A man stopped on the bridge, saw our plight, suggested that I took off my dress, and lay it to dry on the grass. We had both been warned not to talk to strangers, but he seemed genuinely concerned so I did what he said and in a little while we got on our bikes and returned home. Mother soon got me into a hot bath and I felt heaps better.

When I was eight my parents decided to take Rosemary and me on a visit to Ireland. We got on a ferry at Holyhead and travelled at night. It was very exciting going to bed in a bunk! The only other vivid memory of that trip was that World War 2 broke out while we were in Belfast, and the name of Adolf Hitler was on everyone's lips.

(I found out later that my uncle Alan Overton was responsible for helping over two hundred Jewish children, and a few of their parents, to escape from the horrors of Hitler's persecution in the death camps!)

3 WAR TIME

At the age of eight, my perception of war was of course very much influenced by what I heard my parents say. We were all issued with gas masks and a great noisy air-raid siren was installed on the top of the fire station near our shop, its horrible wailing soon became part of our lives. My parents were friendly with the local bank manager and his wife, and they said we could use the underground strong room (with a door 12" thick) as an air-raid shelter. We even had a big bed installed so that we could sleep down there if necessary. Everyone was jumpy and at first there was an uncanny calm settled over the country - the expected air raids did not happen - maybe we even became a bit complacent, until in 1940 all hell broke out. We lived only 10 miles from Coventry, which was the centre of the armament industry. The Nazis decided to do their best to annihilate Coventry and soon we were hearing horror stories of the devastating air raids with people being buried alive in cellars and bank strong rooms and more and more people were homeless. We no longer sheltered in the strong room, but moved to an above ground 'Anderson' shelter in the garden of the Vicarage. I do not remember being very scared except when I saw how scared my father was! Life went on reasonably normally at school, but frequent sessions were spent in the air raid shelters that had ruined our lovely playing field. The 'wailing' would start and we would calmly march across the playground and into the shelter which had concrete benches to sit on. More often than not there was at least 6" of water on the floor so we sat with our feet up on the opposite bench while we sang 'Roll out the barrel', 'Run rabbit run' , and 'Hang out the washing on the Siegfried line'!

The summer of 1940 - as I remember it - was hot and sunny. One Saturday in June my friend Josephine Hobley and I, asked our mums if we could go on a bike ride and picnic together. Our mothers gave permission as long as we were back no later than 7pm. (it did not get dark until after 9pm.) Both of us had small-wheeled children's bikes. The question was where should we go? I'm not sure who suggested it, but we decided to cycle to Coventry to see the bombing!! In the war all the signposts had been taken away (just in case Jerry landed!) so how could we find Coventry? We had no map, but we did have something very helpful - the huge group of barrage balloons in the sky above Coventry. (They were supposed to stop the German planes flying in low by getting tangled in the wires.) So off we set on our small bikes - we left behind the village of Brinklow and with our eyes on the balloons, struck out for our exciting adventure. I still find it hard to believe that we found the energy to cycle that seemingly never-ending 10 miles! At one point we had to carry bikes through a bomb crater in the middle of the road. A little later, we saw a huge red sign on a gate saying UNEXPLODED BOMB - KEEP OUT! We raced over and craned our necks to see if it was anywhere in sight!

Once or twice we felt we had lost our way because the balloons were hidden from view, but we dare not ask anyone in case they thought we were German spies!! At last, we realised that we were on the outskirts of Coventry, but we were not content until we had reached the city centre. A very recent raid had left the huge department store Owen Owens a smouldering ruin. The wax lady models had melted and were sliding down a floor that sloped at an angle of 45 degrees! As we retraced our wheel tracks to the suburbs there were overturned buses, and houses still smoking from the last onslaught, and with hindsight they were probably digging people out too.

We found it all so amazing and I don't think we had any real fear or consciousness of the very real dangers we had exposed ourselves to. (Daylight raids on Coventry were happening frequently.) By this time we were absolutely exhausted, we had no food or drink left and the prospect of the long ride back to Rugby! We were so thirsty that I went and knocked at the door of a nearby house and asked for a glass of water, the lady kindly complied. I arrived back at my house a few minutes before 7pm. My parents were so pleased that I was on time! They asked if we had had a good day - where did we go? I mentioned Brinklow - after all we had passed through it! A year later I said to my mother "You remember the day Jo Hobley and I went on a cycle ride last year? Well if I tell you where we went will you promise not to be cross?" Then it all came out - Mother was speechless - but kept her promise!

1940 was nearly over, in fact it was 5am on Christmas morning. Rosemary and I slept in the same attic bedroom at the top of our three-storey house. Outside our window was a glass roof which allowed light into the shop 30 feet below. Around this skylight was a narrow walkway which led to a series of other roofs and steep drops to the ground. In my Christmas morning excitement, aged 9, I had just asked Romie if I could open my presents yet. She was 15 years old and just as she was saying no it's too early, another voice penetrated our hearing! It was a deep man's voice saying "Goot morning, goot morning." He had a foreign accent and in the dim light of an early winter morning, we could see he was outside our window sitting precariously on the glass roof! Questions flooded our minds, was he a German paratrooper? There had lately been talk of Germans invading by parachute - how else could he have got onto the roof? Surely I of all people should have remembered that it was possible without jumping out of a plane!! After telling him to go back the way he had come, Romie realised she did not want a death on her hands, and she told me to call my parents, but she had difficulty making me hear as I had disappeared under the bedclothes! I ran to the top of the stairs and yelled down "Mummy there's a man up here". I can still see her to this day in her curlers and night-dress rushing up the stairs to confront the intruder. It gradually emerged that he was a Polish Airman, who after a Christmas Eve spree got back very late to the George Hotel next door and found he was locked out. In his alcoholic haze he climbed an eight foot wall, balanced along it to some creeper, climbed that, and inching his way from roof to roof, arrived at our bedroom window, hoping he could get into the hotel and so to bed!! My parents invited him to climb in through the window and they would try to find him a bed for the rest of the night at the local Police Station. The police let him sleep in a cell, and next morning the George Hotel was buzzing with the story of the 'kind people next door who made a poor Polish airman welcome!! (The Polish forces helped this country a lot in the most difficult time of the war).

Although the Coventry bombings were only ten miles away, Rugby was left largely untouched. However, my father was so nervous that he arranged for us to cycle six miles each night to a village called Crick to get away from the bombs! Ironically, a bomb fell nearer to us at Crick than all the time in Rugby! We stayed on a farm with Mr & Mrs. Collett, and at weekends I revelled in the farm life - helping fetch the cows for milking - riding an old lame horse - playing with the many cats and two dogs, and generally feeling part of the Collett family.

When I was nearly 11 years old, my friend and I planned an 'unusual' birthday party. We were allowed to use the two attics, right at the top of our house above the shop (incidentally, parts of the building were over 500 years old with thick walls and bubble glass windows). We wanted to create a 'haunted' house that would scare our friends at my birthday party half to death! One attic was to become an 'operating theatre' - dimly lit, with my friend lying on the bed amongst 'blood' (red ink) stained sheets. I had bought some animals offal from the local butcher, and each guest was invited into the room to observe an operation, with accompanying screams from the patient, and the gory extraction of liver, kidneys, lungs etc. and blood stained medical equipment.

The guest was then ushered into the other attic which was blacked out, and they were escorted over a bridge (plank on two chairs) that crossed a crocodile infested river (bowl of water and appropriate croc. sounds). They then had to pass next to a mad person - growling in a corner (me) and finally - blindfolded, feel a gruesome corpse (my friend) and have their finger plunged into its eye (a lemon). I'm not sure what this episode says about me as a person! I suppose at least it shows initiative and imagination!!

One great consuming passion of my life from very young was dancing. I longed for ballet lessons, and to be a famous ballerina, but was told it was worldly and not right for a Christian. I can still remember the ache of disappointment in my heart. I spent a lot of time on my own, (my sister being so much older), and many an hour was spent dancing to all sorts of music. One day I opened the window in our front upstairs room and danced on a table to the people walking by in the shopping centre, music turned up loud! (the nearest I would ever get to dancing on the stage at Saddlers Wells!)

Years later when I had two young children of my own, I danced to them - the passion was still there and the gift that I had was still largely unfulfilled.

A significant event that occurred in 1941 was my transfer from Northlands School to Rugby High School. It was a rather snobby all girls' school with a very strict and stuffy head mistress who was frightening and remote - as if she was from another world. It was such a contrast from Northlands which had a relaxed atmosphere and where I was always near the top of the class academically. Now I suddenly found that there were others cleverer than I was, and I often came halfway down the list, or lower, when exam results came out. It was a terrible shock, but a worse one had preceded it. Just after taking the scholarship exam for the High School in March, I suddenly became very ill. I had contracted Scarlet Fever and I was so ill that I remember wanting to die.

The newly discovered anti-biotic Penicillin, (which Sir Alexander Fleming had actually discovered in 1928) was only available to troops and not to the general public and Scarlet Fever was a very dangerous disease. I used to peel the skin off my fingers like the fingers of gloves - all in one piece and pile them under my bed!

My parents created an isolation ward for me in one of the attics (it was that or isolation hospital). My lovely curly fair hair was cut off and I lost so much weight that my mother cried when she bathed me. My temperature was 104°F for nearly a week and my throat and mouth were raw and very painful. When I woke in the mornings, my eyes and mouth were stuck together with a horrible thick crust of discharge. I was ill for three months, and when I briefly returned to Northlands before the summer holidays my own teacher did not recognise me!

I recall looking in the mirror one day and realising that I was pale thin and ugly. It was a terrific life shock, but part of a very important humbling of a rather vain little girl. I will always remember how kind Romie was to me when I was so ill. Every day she spent her precious pocket money on a little present to cheer me up.

While talking about my faults! Another incident comes to mind, which illustrates my violent reactions to some people! My great-aunt Belle had invited Rosemary and me to stay with her for a short time at her bungalow in

Welwyn Garden City. She was a very generous person and had bought us many gifts in Marks & Spencer's. However she seemed to be dabbling in spiritualism and just before we went to bed she told us that her dead sister Agnes haunted our bedroom! I was terrified, and this produced a reaction in me so that I took a violent dislike to Aunt Belle, and when I was alone in her kitchen I tore her oilcloth tablecloth in two! When Rosemary saw what I had done she was horrified, but she tried to explain to Aunt Belle that it was an accident! We were never invited back again!!

Meetings at our small Christadelphian Church in Oliver Street, Rugby, took up a significant part of my life. My parents were very much involved with church events, and had a meeting nearly every night of the week. On Sunday, we spent nearly all day at church, Morning service, Sunday School, and evening Gospel lecture. Something seemed to happen to time in those meetings - is it possible that Sunday time goes half as quickly?! I would look up at the clock on the left hand wall, then look away for what seemed ages - but when I looked back the hands didn't seem to have moved at all! Was there ever such a long 40 minutes? Sundays were usually days to dread rather than enjoy. No sewing or knitting or other 'worldly' pursuits, nothing to look forward to - just boring religious games or stories, Thank God that at least mother could make the Bible stories come alive. Mother also ran the large youth club and she produced ' fantastic plays using the whole Sunday School and Youth Club. We performed the life of Esther and Joseph and others, and we did them so well that those who took part never forgot the story or being part of the action! If plays could be such fun why did church itself have to be such a switch off?

After church on Sunday evenings there was always a party at someone's house for the grown-ups - (most often at ours) and we never seemed to be short of food for those special times in spite of food rationing. However, food rationing did have a significant impact on our ordinary everyday life. We had to queue for so many things and people would automatically join a queue if they saw one forming, sometimes not even knowing what they were queuing for until they got to the front with some quite amusing results at times. Like the man who joined a queue only to find that he had been queuing for women's underwear! The government took early action to bring in rationing which ensured that basic essentials were available to all, in fact the diet in the war was quite a healthy one and we all had enough to eat.

Luxuries disappeared such as bananas grapes and pineapples. Cakes were made with dried eggs and were a revolting bright shade of yellow. Biscuits were a rare treat, margarine (which tasted like axle grease) replaced butter. Fresh eggs were a rarity and we had 2oz of meat each a week! (The black marketeers did well!) Sweets were rationed, but we had much better teeth as a result! Rationing did not finish until well after the war was over.

I remember one Sunday evening on the six o'clock news it was announced that clothes would be rationed from the next day, and that at first (until clothes coupons were printed) bread coupons would be used. The women in the church seemed particularly friendly to my parents all of a sudden and they came in swarms to our shop that night to buy dresses and coats and undies before the rationing started the next day! We did very well out of the war!

By the end of 1944, the war seemed to be going our way and Hitler was on the run. My father and mother decided to have a look at the Isle of Wight as a possible place to live and find a bit more sunshine, not to mention being by the seaside! In order to even visit the Island father had to obtain a police permit because the south coast was a restricted area, all prepared for an invasion by the Germans. Piers had had their middle sections removed - there was barbed wire along all the promenades and beaches, and great concrete blocks everywhere. Gun emplacements were at every vantage point. Father started visiting the Isle of Wight at regular intervals to see about buying a shop and a house. Eventually he found a shop in a good position in Sandown High Street.

Then my father took me with him to the Island in the search for a house. I remember the police officer at Ryde looking at me and then saying 'Hello Mr. Thorneloe, back again and who is this young lady?' I wondered if he would refuse permission for me to land, as I did not have a permit! However, so much for my childish self-importance, there was no problem! We went to see this amazing house on the Broadway, it was called "Kintore" and had seven bedrooms, a tower, a huge garden, an orchard and stables. It had not been lived in for years - the garden was overgrown and the horses had fled! The rooms had dark brown wallpaper and gas lighting - no electricity, but it had a wonderful wide staircase with a shiny banister, and a summerhouse in the garden. It also had a large cellar and of course the tower - from which you could see the sea if you stood on tiptoe!

I was so excited at the prospect of living in such a place after all my life living over the shop in Rugby. We could imagine how it would look with light paint and electric lights. We loved the large conservatory with its neglected grapevines, which went round two sides of the house. Father made an offer and it was accepted, £1200 a bargain even in 1944, (now in 1996 worth £500,000 at least!). We went home, described the house to mother and Rosemary, and started to make plans for our move in October.

In the interval between us deciding to move to the Isle of Wight and actually going, D-Day occurred. The Isle of Wight was of course in a strategic position and there were some amazing discoveries made by us on arrival in the Island. One big challenge for the war department was how to refuel all the army vehicles once they had landed on the coast of France, so they devised an ingenious plan which they called PLUTO - pipe line under the ocean! The huge pipelines went from Sandown beach and Shanklin pier. When out walking one day, my father and I discovered the Sandown one with its small pool of leaked oil hidden in the grass on the way to Culver cliff. By this time D-Day was in the past, but amongst the islanders the whole project had been a closely guarded 'open' secret for months!

We had a narrow area of beach (about 50 yards wide) where we were allowed to bathe. All the rest of the beach was mined and covered with barbed wire. A flying bomb (doodlebug) had fallen at the village of Lake causing devastation, but now the war was virtually over. I cut out the maps from the newspapers as the allies advanced on Berlin. (I still have those maps!). President Roosevelt died on April 12 and tragically missed the end of the war, (it is almost certain that if President Roosevelt had not helped this country secretly in the early 40s Hitler would have invaded Britain).

4 TEENAGE YEARS.

About this time, I became quite boy mad! Looking back in my diary, I find a different boy's name every few weeks! When I was about fourteen I used to go to stay with Romie (who was now living with Auntie Lily and Uncle Hubert in Croydon), and it was Romie who showed me how to put on make-up. She was by this time going out with Roger Humphrys her future husband, and he had a friend called Julian Yockney. So, Romie arranged for the four of us to go out together while I was on a short visit to London. Julian was five years older than I was and he quite swept me off my feet. He made me feel very special, especially when he kissed me in the moonlight under Westminster Bridge. When I got home, I very soon received a letter from Julian asking when he could see me next. A few weeks later I asked if I could go to London again to see Romie! My parents, not suspecting the real reason, gladly gave permission.

It was on this occasion that Julian asked me to marry him! He said he would like to take me to live in Canada as soon as I got my parents consent. On looking back, I am amazed that neither of us seemed to consider the fact of me being only 14 years of age and Julian 19 an obstacle! When our romance came to the notice of both sets of parents, they exchanged letters and made it very difficult for us to meet, and unlike Romeo and Juliet, the flame of passion was soon extinguished! However, for a short time I really did feel as if my heart would break.

Many years later, I met Julian again, this time I was accompanied by Phil. The rosy memories of my first love were quickly shattered, and I thanked God for such a merciful escape when I saw what Julian had become. One very positive thing came out of my visits to London was the growing friendship that developed between Rosemary and me. The six year gap seemed to diminish and now we were two grownups together, or that's what I told myself, at fourteen I felt I had left childhood far behind!

Sandown Grammar School was five minutes run (and I mean on foot) from Kintore. It was an ancient building with dark staircases and funny old-fashioned classrooms, some of which were part of the assembly hall and they were created by unfolding half glass partition doors. The science labs had the smell of chemicals that seemed to permeate the very fabric from when the school was built! In spite of being in a very beautiful rural part of Sandown, there was no playing field attached to the school, but was half a mile away, and there was not even a decent gymnasium. I was passionate about sport, particularly swimming, including life saving, and hockey. Eventually I got into the first eleven.

I can still remember the day when I first nervously walked those few yards from home. I knew I would be the only new girl (as it was half term) and horror of horrors there would be boys in the class! I walked into the classroom and was the focus for every pair of eyes. One of the boys made a pair of spectacles out of wire, and putting them on his nose said "What's that peculiar insect that has just walked in?" The girls were friendly and helped me

to feel better and within a few days the boy's teasing was more good-humoured.

In fact, I became so fascinated with the males that I soon found it difficult to concentrate on boring old school work. I had started to get invitations to go out with various ones, but fairly soon four of us were inseparable and remained so throughout our school lives. Two boys, David and Alan, and Nancy and I went everywhere together, not as sweethearts but as close friends. We cycled, swam, walked, went to pictures, and talked - later David and I became particularly close and some heartache followed, but it was all very innocent and harmless. I did have other 'dates' and some were more risky than I realised in my naivety. As I look back, I thank God for his protection on many occasions.

My parents had no idea what was going on, but at one point they suspected that I was seeing boys outside of school time and they forbade me to ever go out with anyone. That simply drove the whole thing further underground and did not help me at all. If only they had been willing to talk to me in an understanding and adult manner. However, I realise that bringing me up was not easy, and I know they sincerely wanted the best for me because they loved me.

While the challenge of being a teenager was happening to me, my love of Jesus and my desire to serve him increased. To my amazement, my parents allowed me to join a youth club in Sandown. I think they realised I was lonely except when I was at school.

At the youth club I became friendly with a girl called Betty and I discovered she went to a nearby Anglican Church. We had lots of chats about religion and one day when she was at our house she produced a list of questions which her vicar had given her to ask us when he heard that she was friendly with a Christadelphian! I can still remember how uncomfortable I felt as my father attempted to answer the challenging questions about the devil, the Trinity etc. etc. Even at that age I was starting to question why Christadelphians seemed to mess around with scripture to avoid the obvious interpretation of passages such as John chapter 1. The seeds were sown during that encounter with Betty, which would many years later result in a parting of the ways from the Christadelphians.

I often talked to my friends about my faith, and some of them came to our little church service, which was held at Kintore. It was so much better to have church in the informal atmosphere of our lounge than in a cold austere hall, and visitors often came across from the mainland in the summer months. I decided that I wanted to be baptised when I was 15 to the delight of my parents. They arranged for some brothers from the Christadelphian church in Portsmouth to come across to test my knowledge of scripture! The examination lasted for three hours, and covered such things as - who were the kings of Israel and Judah and why did Jesus need to die for himself?!

I don't remember any mention being made of the need for me to confess and repent of my sins, or the need to receive forgiveness and enter into salvation. In spite of this I believe my baptism on the following Sunday morning at Portsmouth Christadelphian Hall was a very important day in my life. God was already working in me by His Holy Spirit, although I didn't know it or even believe in the Holy Spirit in those days. That decision was an anchor in the turbulent days and months that followed.

The next three years were in general happy ones at school home and church, then came the decision whether to stay on at school or go into the family business. All my close friends were leaving school so the incentive to stay on and pursue my ambition to  become a sports teacher was not great enough to withstand the pressure to conform to family plans. (Later I would deeply regret my weak decision and the lack of encouragement by my parents to go to college, but now I realise that I must take at least 50% of the blame).

As I look back, I thank God for my parents profound influence on my life. Father was a man of integrity in his personal life and in the way he ran his businesses, in spite of numerous temptations to take short cuts and get involved in dishonest practices. Mother had a tender, sensitive heart and a deep concern for people. One phrase she often used has come back to me and helped throughout my life "People are more important than things". Almost every day as I left for school she would say A.U.T.L. which stood for As Unto The Lord. There were occasions when this ritual irritated me, but because it was said from the sincerity of mother's love for Jesus, it did have an effect on my thinking and attitudes.

5 AUSTRALIA – THE GREAT ADVENTURE!

Once I had left school, the Isle of Wight became a lonely and rather boring place for me as a 17-year-old. My friends had gone to the mainland to pursue their careers. There were no young people at church and going for walks on Sunday along the cliffs with my parents was not my idea of fun, so I was delighted when my parents decided to explore the idea of going to live in Australia!

Trips to Australia House in London followed and then we were told we would have to wait at least six months for a passage. It was 1948 and British people were eagerly accepting the governments offer of passages to Australia for £10 each - understandable after five years of bombs rationing and the English climate. I had been in charge of a teenage clothes shop that father had bought on Shanklin High Street. It was one of the first shops in the country devoted to special clothes for teenagers! We sold up everything in Sandown and Shanklin and moved for the few months before going to Australia, to live with my aunt and uncle at Gravesend in Kent.

While living with them I worked at John Lewis in Oxford St. and travelled each day quite a long journey by train and tube to the West End. I loved being part of the London scene even the rush hour! I soon made some good friends amongst my colleagues and we went in groups from work to see operas and ballets at Covent Garden and Saddlers Wells. I even saw Moira Shearer dance before she became famous in the film "The Red Shoes."

I did well at John Lewis and was soon offered a small department to run myself! I even did some modelling of new lines and had to go up and show them to the General Manager Mr. Dawson feeling rather embarrassed because most of them had rather low necks!!

Another occasion that I met the General Manager face to face was when I was accused of theft!! A customer had rung up and suggested that I had stolen some of her clothing coupons which she adamantly declared she had given me several weeks before when she bought a dress. I was told about this by a section manager and that I had to go and see Mr. Dawson. I could not remember anything at all about the customer or the incident. All I knew was that I had not stolen her wretched coupons. As I climbed the stairs to the General Managers office I felt my face going red and was convinced he would think I was guilty. It was a horrible experience but he was very understanding and said "Don't worry Miss Thorneloe, customers often try this sort of thing, we trust you and are convinced you have told the truth."

I was quite sad to leave John Lewis's when at last our booking came through to sail on the S.S. Largs Bay to Melbourne on February 26th 1949. What a strange feeling it was to leave all that is familiar and to sail half way around the world to an unknown continent. At age 18, there was a different edge to it I suppose. A sense of anticipation about the future combined with living very much for each day. Life on board ship was full of excitement (once the initial seasickness in the Mediterranean was over).

There were only about half a dozen eligible young girls amongst the 250 passengers so we came in for a fair amount of attention from the officers and crew. It was a heady experience and one that I was ill equipped to cope with. Previously my boyfriends had been immature schoolboys, with the exception of Julian Yockney. Now on board ship - miles from land, the ship was a law unto itself, and I was thrust into a world of sophistication and temptation. What could be more alluring than a handsome officer in his summer white uniform seeming to imply that I was the centre of his world!

What could be more naive than me, an 18 year old girl dressing up for the fancy dress dance as an eastern dancing girl, black satin trousers bare midriff, see-through veils, jewellery - the whole bit, being surprised that I was invited to the officers quarters for a drink! Not, as I was led to believe, to the bar, but to his cabin.

As soon as he shut and locked the door I was filled with panic and fear, suddenly realising his intentions. Only a miracle could save me (I have many many times since, thanked God with all my heart that He cared about me and protected me in my youthful foolishness.) As things were hotting up, there was a knock at the cabin door and a semi-drunk officer barged in, much to the anger of 'my' officer. I fled and was on the top deck within seconds, nearly fainting with relief.

Our ports of call were fascinating and glamorous, first we called at Malta, then Port Said in Egypt, and Aden. Passing through the Suez Canal was amazing, we went in a convoy, only just room for the ship, sometimes touching the sides. We saw the incredible white De Lessups monument which was blown up a few weeks later in the Ishmaeleer war. One day as we sailed into the Red sea, mother excitedly pointed out Mount Sinai on our left hand side. We also saw the wells of the Queen of Sheba on a trip from Aden where little boys dived in off the bridge to retrieve coins that we tourists threw into the mud! It was all so hot and different from anything I had ever seen. Native people swarmed onto the ship to sell us their wares, everyone had to barter, and the locals still did well because of our ignorance.

After Aden, with its goats in the streets and veiled women, we were at sea for seven days before we arrived at Colombo in Ceylon, and had a wonderful trip to Mount Lavinia. The women in Ceylon were so beautiful in their saris and gorgeous brown skin, they made us English girls look quite insipid. After Ceylon we crossed the equator and endured the King Neptune ceremony, which was good fun.

Ten days after leaving Colombo we reached the West Coast waters of Australia! Mother called me up on deck and said "Come and smell Australia!" Sure enough, wafting on the wind was the faint aroma of eucalyptus!

Some Christadelphians met us at Fremantle and we stayed with the Tuckers who were very warm and friendly. Perth is a beautiful city on the wide Swan River. Everything was so different and glamorous, - hot weather, spider drinks, milkshakes, flashing neon signs, no rationing, the totally different animals, birds and trees, the smell of eucalyptus, swimming and going prawning in the river! We were forced to stay ten days at Perth because of the Fremantle dock strike, but we didn't mind, it was a brilliant opportunity to see a little more of Western Australia, and make some friends amongst the young people in Perth. We sailed on to Adelaide and met more friendly Christadelphians. By this time, we were very keen to reach our destination.

The photo below was taken shortly after our arrival in Australia.

6 FALLING IN LOVE.

It was April 13, 1949, and at last the time came for us to land in Melbourne and to leave the ship that had been our home for seven weeks. Again we were met by people from the church and taken to their home. Australians are very friendly and hospitable people who do not stand on ceremony, if they say drop in when you are passing they mean it and are not just being polite! While my parents hunted for a house to buy we were looked after for several weeks by Robert and Rhoda Walker. They took us to see many local beauty spots and gave us a great time.

On April 23 - just ten days after arriving in Melbourne - I met the young man I was going to marry! It was a warm Saturday afternoon, and I had been invited, along with about 30 others to celebrate Brenda Hardy's 21st birthday. Her parents had hired a hall in Moorabbin, an outer suburb of Melbourne, and it was close to the railway station. A group of us went round to meet the train that most of the guests were coming on, (I found out later that it was at the station Phil first noticed me). I was rather apprehensive at being the new girl and meeting all these young folks for the first time. Just before we sat down for the meal, I remember noticing a handsome young man in a brown suit leaning up against a wall talking to a friend. He was the one that seemed to stand out in the crowd, little did I realise that in just over a year, we would be married!!

Brenda and Ron (her boyfriend) had deliberately arranged that I would sit by Phil Hawkins at the meal, they knew that his longstanding romance with Alma McGregor had recently finished and they wanted to cheer him up! It was not easy to get Phil to talk, as he was the strong silent type, but that attracted me to him even more! Soon after the meal, we had a game that required partners, and an unusual way had been devised to pair people off. All the girls had to remove their shoes - hide one behind them and put the others in a sack. The guys then rummaged in the sack for a shoe and tried to find their " Cinderella "! Phil dived in and immediately pulled out mine - he came straight to me and he had his partner. He had no trouble recognising my shoe, it was the only one in the sack with 4" heels a thick platform sole

and two ankle straps - a London fashion that had not yet reached the antipodes!

The game we were partnered for was as follows - everyone had lots of newspapers and pins from which they had to try to make an outfit - the best effort won, I don't recall that it was us, but it was great fun trying. Phil and I remained partners for the rest of the evening, which delighted me as I was already looking forward to being escorted home by Phil. Then I noticed Ian McGregor (Alma's brother) go up to him and whisper something in his ear. I later found out that he had said "I'm taking Jose home". It was with a keen sense of disappointment that I accepted Ian's offer when it became obvious that Phil was not going to ask me himself.

So the course of true love was dramatically diverted into a whirlwind romance with Ian, a very forceful character! We went out together almost every day and I was mesmerised by this good-looking dark-haired extrovert. He was diametrically opposite in personality to Phil, and in my heart of hearts I knew he was not good for me, and not really a Christian in spite of suddenly coming to all the church meetings. My parents certainly did not approve of Ian and as they had not yet found a suitable house to buy in Melbourne, they quickly bought a caravan in order to tour N.S.W. and Queensland and get me away from Ian!

Our tour of the East Coast was limited somewhat by the fact that petrol was rationed in May 1949, so we only had enough to get to Toowoomba, just North of Brisbane. On the way, we saw the comparatively new capital city of Canberra with its gleaming white buildings and recently planted trees. I remember how in the evenings the possums used to scrabble around on the roof of the caravan, and in the daytime the kookaburras would line up on the washing lines and trees and laugh their heads off at us! (We grew to love these friendly overgrown 'kingfishers').

On we travelled to Sydney and then North up the Gold Coast and all the surfing beaches. I made friends with the lifeguards at Surfers' Paradise and they kept calling for me at the caravan, but met with a cool reception from my parents. However, I saw them when I went swimming and the memory of Ian was fading fast.

The roads between the large cities were mostly rough gravel with ruts and potholes, which sometimes made travelling difficult. Amazingly however, father let me drive our big American Oldsmobile towing the caravan quite often and I even hit 60 mph a few times! We went to all the Christadelphian Churches on the way and met a wide variety of people young and old, nice and not so nice. Father spent a lot of time trying to persuade the different fellowships to be reunited. (They were divided into the Central and the Shield fellowships.) Father was a peace maker, and eventually a few years later, his and a few others efforts, were at last rewarded when there was a reunion after 50 years at enmity with each other!

We were now coming to the end of our petrol coupons, so we had to start back to Melbourne, our new home. On the way through N.S.W. we saw the beautiful Blue Mountains, and then we came to Maitland, only to find that nearly the whole town was under flood water - those poor people! We had to take a very long diversion to get back onto the main road.

Wednesday June 29, it was good to be back, and my parents efforts to take my mind off Ian had worked! I now saw him in a different light and avoided getting involved again in spite of very strong urgings from Ian and his family. It was in the McGregor house, at a party, that I saw Phil again, and that old feeling of attraction to him came back but nothing happened. Robert Walker, with whom we were staying until the purchase of our house, at 3 Scott's Parade, Ivanhoe, was completed, offered me a job in his Coburg store, until the time when father also settled on a shop for me to manage. I enjoyed the work a lot and soon was given more responsibilities.

By mid August, my longing to get to know Phil better had grown and grown, and I was thrilled when one Sunday, Mother, Father, and I were invited to have a meal with the Hawkins family. Early in September, Phil and I sat together at a Youth Concert in Melbourne Town Hall, and he took me home afterwards. From this time on, my thoughts rarely left the subject of Phil Hawkins, and at last I was beginning to know what it was to be really deeply in love with a person, and not just an idea. The more we talked, the more we found we had in common and it was thrilling to be together. We never ran out of interesting things to talk about, and there was a sort of serene certainty that this relationship was not going to end, that it would grow and flourish and deepen every day of our lives. We were a passionate young couple, and there were times when self control was far from easy, but each of us wanted to save ourselves for our wedding day, and to honour what we knew God wanted for our lives.

The year 1949 ended with a family camp at Port Arlington on Port Phillip Bay. It was on January 6 1950 that Phil asked me to marry him, exactly one year to the day before our actual wedding! I was 18 years old and Phil was 22, and we knew with certainty that there could be no one else for either of us, so of course I said yes! It was another matter to persuade my father that I was ready for marriage at 18. He said wait until you are 21 and my heart sank, but mother was my ally and after she had talked to father he changed his mind and gave permission for us to become engaged.

About a year after we moved to Australia, my sister and Roger and their little baby Katy, arrived by ship. I shall always remember how wonderful it was to see them after a year's separation. They settled in a house at Box Hill. The following year, Phil graduated from Melbourne University and he applied for teaching jobs throughout the state of Victoria. Jobs in Melbourne had been at the top of his list, but because he was a young newly qualified teacher, he was automatically posted to a country town Secondary School at Bendigo, 98 miles north of Melbourne. A one-time famous gold mining town Bendigo, together with its sister city Ballarat, where the only civil war in Australian history was fought at Eureka Stockade!

7 EARLY MARRIED LIFE.

At last January 6 1951 came, gloriously hot and sunny, by midday over 100 degrees in the shade! .My white diaphanous, broderie anglaise wedding dress looked cool and beautiful and was just right for a teenage bride weighing 7st. 8oz! Phil's sister Miriam had expertly made it, and Phil's wedding suit! (She was a tailoress). At 10 a.m. we were legally married at Melbourne Register Office, with just a few close family present, and then we drove to our church hall where all the guests were waiting, and during a lovely service, we said these precious vows to each other.

I call upon these persons here present to witness that I Jose Thorneloe, do take thee, Phil Hawkins, to be my lawful wedded husband, to have and to hold from this day forward, for better for worse, for richer for poorer, in sickness and in health, to love and to cherish, till death us do part, according to God's holy law, and to this I pledge myself.

As we looked around the tables at our wedding breakfast, we were suddenly aware of how much our parents had done for us throughout our lives - so much love and care. Above all, I look back with gratitude that they had taught us to love God. Jesus had always been a vivid, dynamic person to me, thanks to my mother's enthusiasm and her own personal relationship with Him, that was a very precious legacy.

Eventually the farewells were said, and we were driven to Melbourne airport where we boarded a Dakota plane for Hobart Tasmania. It was my first flight, and I was fairly apprehensive, but being with my new husband quite took my mind off the possibility of a crash!

I now want to give a snapshot of the twelve months from our marriage to the birth of our beloved first born son Laurie - filling in some details of life in Kangaroo Flat later.

I doubt if there could have been a less prepared teenage bride. Married at nineteen, with a mother who was too embarrassed to talk about sex, one older sister, and no brothers, my preparedness was based on a few rather boring biology lessons (plus diagrams!), and a deep and passionate love for my handsome and loving husband, Phil. His family being even more puritanical in attitude than mine, made us an ideal combination for honeymoon disaster! If our love had not been so strong, and his patience and tenderness so amazing, our marriage could well have been finished that very first week!

We did not really want a family immediately because we were almost penniless! We hadn't a home, just one room in a bad-tempered old man's house - he made our lives a misery. No one advised us, no one suggested what we could do to avoid having children until we could at least afford some nappies! No one bothered to share some of their experiences, gained through mistakes and triumphs, no one warned us of some of the pitfalls of early married life - like comparing my father's abilities (learnt over many years), with those of my husband.

Of course, it was inevitable that I became pregnant during the second week of our honeymoon (it would have been virtually impossible before!). I didn't even realise I was pregnant until two months later, when I suddenly became very ill and lost my tiny unacknowledged baby. Very soon after that I must have become pregnant again, and almost a year to the day from our marriage, I gave birth to our elder son Laurence.

I had tried to find out what it would be like to give birth. Everyone was evasive and non-committal. As far as I know there were no antenatal classes to go to, no recommended exercises, no indicators about the beautiful miracle that was happening inside me during those nine months. I was robbed, by ignorance, of the thrill and excitement of following each fascinating stage in the development of our child.

The first contraction arrived - at least I did know what that meant! After about seven hours, my mother (in whose house we were staying), persuaded me to go to the hospital, and at 5pm Phil reluctantly handed me over to the nurse in charge. It was unthinkable, in those days that my husband could be with me at a time when I most needed him, and that he could witness one of the most wonderful events in creation. So the longest and loneliest night of my life commenced. Left completely alone (except for brief periodic visits and examinations by nursing staff), I was frightened and ignorant and dazed with the worst pain I had ever experienced in my life.

Illogically, I felt betrayed by all the women in the world who had not even hinted what I was to expect. I watched the clock's hands turning, minute by minute, hour by hour, and it was obvious even to me, that this birth was taking far too long, and that no real progress was being made. Thirty six hours had passed since the first contraction. Suddenly there was an atmosphere of panic in the room. The female doctor didn't seem to know what to do, (I sensed that in my stupor). Then the smell of ether in my nose and mouth - no communication, just unconsciousness. Heavy eyed and bewildered I heard voices - "You have a son" - I did not believe them until I was conscious of a tiny head against my cheek - my very own child, such overwhelming joy and gratitude!

Two days passed, no one told me why I was not allowed to see my own son, and no one explained why everyone else held their babies and fed them but they never brought my son to me... Each night I cried myself to sleep, worrying about my baby and not daring to ask what was wrong. It was not until later that I found that he had been so badly knocked about with the forceps that they decided he could not be moved. At last, they brought him to me, his head all misshapen and bruised from the forceps, which had dragged him into the world. Nine days later I left hospital, no one had shown me how to bath or change my son's nappy, and I was too timid to ask, so I went back to my parent's home in total ignorance of even the basic practical ingredients of motherhood! It was assumed that giving birth would automatically give me the answers!

All this happened many years ago in Melbourne Australia, and I still find it hard to forgive the way my son and I were treated in 1952. (in fact even writing this down has caused a welling up of emotion). I believe that the traumatic birth must have had a deep effect on my son and me, but more than that, the totally unnecessary two day separation during the vital time when bonding should have been reinforced, had a profound effect upon our early relationship.

So why rake all this up when it happened so long ago, and it all sounds so negative? I suppose it is because to encourage young women who live now, to enjoy being mothers in this amazing and more enlightened age, and to remind ourselves of the wonderful discoveries and facilities that can make pregnancy and motherhood an even more exciting and fascinating experience than it was in the past.

Hundreds of years ago King David wrote

"O Lord, you have examined my heart and know everything about me. You made all my delicate, inner parts of my body, and knit them together in my mother's womb. Thank you for making me so wonderfully complex! It is amazing to think about. Your workmanship is marvellous - and how well I know it. You were there when I was being formed in utter seclusion! You saw me before I was born and scheduled each day of my life before I began to breathe. Every day was recorded in your Book!"

Psalm 139 (Living Bible).

I can't help wondering how David would feel if he could look down a microscope and see things he had not even dreamed of, or watch a modern film of life in the womb from conception to birth, or hear the recorded sounds of mother's voice as baby hears it! Surely, he would be lost in wonder love and praise!

The early months of our marriage in Kangaroo Flat - a small township 4 miles south of Bendigo, - were a mixture of great joy, some real challenges as two opposites tried to co-exist, and great loneliness for me. We still marvel at the stupidity of me not getting a job while I waited for Laurie to be born. It would certainly have helped with finances, we hardly had a penny, and I would not have had to endure twelve months of extreme loneliness, while Phil was at work, (I remember longing for Laurie to be born so that I would have someone to talk to!).

By the time Laurie was on the way, we had moved into a new house, 35 Wesley St., which we had persuaded the Education Department to buy, so that we could rent it from them. This was to be our home for nearly four years. Even though it was a new house (we had watched it being built), there never were any sewerage or drains laid while we lived there. Our 'toilet' was a small shed down the garden with a container under the seat, which was collected once a week by opening a flap at the back - woe betide you if you happened to be sitting on the throne when the man came!

We had no furniture at all, and very little money to buy any, so I went to an auction in Bendigo and bought a lounge suite for £17, and a table and four chairs - I can't remember how much they cost! When we got the lounge suite home we discovered that it smelt revoltingly of cats! We put it outside, scrubbed it with disinfectant, and left it to dry in the hot sun, it was as good as new! (well nearly!). We had no electricity for six months and managed with oil lamps. The only way to cook, to heat the place, and to have baths, was to go out in the 'bush' and gather timber which we piled into the back of our ancient jalopy - 1934 Standard with "dickey" at the back and soft roof. We were soft in the head to buy it, they must have seen us coming!!! In the kitchen was a one-fire stove, saucepans were heated on the top, burning wood in the middle cupboard, and the oven at the bottom. We had no hot water except what we heated on the stove. I could cook a delicious roast dinner on the top shelf of the oven while cooking meringues in the bottom, the temperature was so variable.

It took well over an hour to run a bath, because the bath heater consisted of a metal cylinder with a jacket of water around it, and a space underneath into which you fed small chips of wood! The bottom of the bath was open to the elements, and in the winter, it got cold in Bendigo, (near to freezing some nights) so  as the bath water ran in it would cool down rapidly! As a result, bath night was not very frequent! More often than not, we would stand in the baby's bath in the kitchen to have a wash-down in front of the kitchen stove.

One evening, I was standing 'starkers' in the baby bath, when a knock came at the back door two feet from where I stood! Remember we were at the back of beyond, and not expecting visitors. I grabbed a towel and dashed out of the room leaving a trail of wet footprints as Phil let in a Life Insurance agent who had trudged all the way out to Kangaroo flat, and Phil tried to get rid of him as soon as possible! not easy!

Once a fortnight Phil and I would take Laurie out to the bush (with our five-shilling licence), to collect timber for our home. Laurie loved to help his daddy, and would struggle to drag long branches to the car, if we tried to help him he would say, "I'll do it! I'll do it!" Whenever Phil serviced the car, Laurie was always there fetching and handing him tools.

I shall never forget the day when I went outside, and noticed that Laurie was playing with an old bucket that the builders had left. I glanced into the bucket and to my horror saw several red-back spiders. (The Australian red-back spider is deadly to children and causes severe illness to adults - it is only small, about half an inch across its jet black body with a vivid red stripe unmistakable!) The thought that Laurie could so easily have died set me shaking with horror! I rushed into the kitchen, grabbed the DDT spray, and with a trembling hand sprayed until the little 'monsters' were dead. When Phil got home and heard what had happened, he went and looked at the pile of builder's rubble at the side of the garden and found it was infested with red-backs! ... We soon got rid of that death-trap too.

Not long after that, I was hanging out nappies on our clothesline, which was tied to a Gum tree at the far end of the garden. As I brushed against the tree, I felt a sharp stab into my right arm. I looked down and saw blood oozing out of a double incision. My immediate thought was, a snake had bitten me. Most Australian snakes are deadly - some within a matter of minutes. Trembling with fear as I watched my arm swell up, I dashed into the house, it was the weekend, and Phil was at home. Needing to know the source of the poison in order to treat it, Phil rushed to the tree - he found no sign of a snake, but he discovered a large vivid green caterpillar with pincer-like horns on its back which it brought together to inflict a double incision as it injected poison into the flesh!! Frightening but not fatal! The swelling soon went down, as did my heart rate, so I live to tell the tale!

On Sundays, we went into Bendigo on the tram, in order to get another tram out to Cal Gully, the gold mining part of Bendigo. All over the place were the poppet legs of the mines, and underneath our feet were numerous passages and shafts, (some half a mile deep) of the old mine workings. The Deborah mine was still working in our time, whereas now it is a model mine for visitors. The reason we were making this weekly journey to Cal Gully, was to visit an elderly Christadelphian gold mine manager's widow called Sarah McClelland. She still lived in the mine manager's house. It was large and forbidding, every blind pulled down to keep out the relentless, dazzling sunlight.

On our first visit, I remember we knocked at the door, were ushered into the dark corridors blinded by the darkness after the brilliant hot January sun. A 'servant' took us to a large bedroom - and as our eyes gradually became accustomed to the darkness, we saw a huge bed with a very old woman in it. She had long white hair and pale skin - all it needed to complete the Dickensian allusion, was a rotting bridal dress and a rat infested wedding cake! She asked the servant to raise the blind a little - i.e. one inch!, and she then indicated her pleasure that we had bothered to call on her. As we were talking, we heard a distant sound of shuffling and bumping as of a heavy weight being laboriously dragged towards the bedroom. Sarah showed no shock as the noise got nearer, in fact she told us it was her daughter Topsy. Into the dimly lit room came a grotesque sight - a woman of fortyish on crutches, body badly deformed and contorted, face twisted and ugly. We were introduced and with difficulty, she talked to us. It soon became clear that there was absolutely nothing wrong with her mental capacity, and she even taught the piano to several local children!

So began our acquaintance with the McClellands. Every Sunday we went to have communion with Sarah McClelland and to keep her company. Topsy never came in, but sat listening outside the room. After about a year, the old lady died, and Christadelphians from Melbourne travelled the hundred miles to conduct the funeral. On the way back to the house after the funeral, Topsy said, "I suppose you won't be coming to visit on a Sunday now". We asked her what she would like us to do and discovered she wanted us to continue our visits, which we gladly did. Some weeks, Phil would fetch her to our house in our old jalopy, carrying her in and out of the car, (she was very heavy). One Sunday as Phil brought Topsy to have lunch with us, she said "My mother's dearest wish was that I would be baptised; would you and Jo talk to me about Jesus?" I hardly need to say how thrilled we were, but as we listened to Topsy we realised how much anger she felt towards God because of her condition, (understandably of course). All those weeks when we had visited her mother and talked about Jesus, she had been listening outside in the other room, and something was kindled in heart. Gradually we saw the bitterness and anger go, and a desire came to commit her life to the one who loved her so much and would one day free her from her terrible bondage. She was baptised in the bath in our home at Kangaroo Flat to our great joy and thankfulness.

Through Topsy we discovered six other Christadelphians who lived in and around Bendigo, and so a small church began in our house every Sunday. Even though I was barely out of my teens, and Phil 23, and they were much older, they expected us to lead the church! It proved a very challenging role to take on, with family rivalries and jealousies rearing their heads amongst the older folks, our baptism of fire you might say! On a lighter note, Phil and I with Laurie, often used to go out for picnics, and swimming outings, and one day when we were sitting on the bank of a river near Ballarat, we were thrilled to see a duck-billed platypus swimming near us!

During our four years in Bendigo, we made friends with several members of staff at Bendigo High School, and they used to spend evenings with us, we played card games and had a great laugh. Most of them were single young men far from home. I was invited to join the Bendigo Ex High

School girls hockey team, which involved going to practises before breakfast! I got to know lots of the High School students there, and at the school dances. I was about the same age as some of the sixth formers! A couple of times a week, I would go the four miles into Bendigo to take Laurie to the Health Centre, look at the shops and meet Phil out of school.

When Laurie was fifteen months old, I discovered I was pregnant again, at first it was a shock, we were so hard up! but we soon began to look forward eagerly to "Susie" being born. By coincidence, we were again to be in Melbourne for the long school summer holidays, so we booked into a private Nursing Home (near my parents' house in a suburb of Melbourne called Brighton). It was called Araluen, whereas the Nursing Home where Laurie was born in Ivanhoe, was called Airlie, never to be forgotten!

January is not a good month to give birth in Australia! It was well over 100 degrees F. when Laurie was born, and when I went into labour with Vicki Jo, (Susie no longer seemed to fit!) it was over 109°F.

Phil stayed with me for a while, but much to both our regret now, not until her birth. This time the process took 36 hours rather than 48 hours with Laurie, so I suppose that was an improvement! I had a lovely nurse named Sister Churchwood, she was so loving and kind. She spent a lot of time mopping my head and cooling me down with wet flannels. Doctor Farrell popped in and was sure Vicki would be born by midnight on Australia Day January 26th, in which case we would have been given a silver spoon to celebrate, but she was actually born 3.45am on January 27th. As she came into the world, there was a short panic because the cord was tightly around her neck, and at first she did not breathe. They acted quickly and efficiently, and I was soon relieved to hear her lusty cries. She was so pretty, even at birth, my darling daughter Vicki, dark hair and eyes, and a lovely shapely head. My biggest concern was being separated from Laurie. I missed him terribly, and Mother and Father were wonderful with him, but he was upset and confused by my sudden disappearance, even though we had all tried to explain to him what was happening. The worst thing was, that the Nursing Home people had a policy of not allowing children to visit - not even brothers and sisters of new babies! On the fourth day, I was allowed to go out into the garden, and I shall never forget the look on Laurie's face, when he came in the gate and saw me - we both cried with joy. Laurie had some difficulty accepting his new sister, and in the car going back to the house, he would not look at her or touch her. However very soon that afternoon, he started hugging and kissing her. I never remember any time from then on, when Laurie and Vicki did not have a loving and positive relationship. They were the best of friends and rarely quarrelled or were unkind to each other.

Six months after Vicki's birth, my darling Phil landed up in the same hospital. After a night of excruciating pain, he was rushed in by Dr. Farrell (who had delivered Vicki), for a complicated three hour operation, to remove a 'near to bursting' appendix. It was a terrible experience for him, but we thank God for the skill of dear Dr. Farrell who played a vital part in both our lives.

When Vicki was only six months old, she became seriously ill with Bronchitis, we were very worried about her and I wrote and told mother and father, (writing was our main form of communication). Two days later, just after breakfast, I went out to our post-box which was attached to the front gate, to see if there were any letters. I glanced up the dusty track which led to Kangaroo Flat, our nearest village, and to my astonishment and joy I saw mother walking towards me! I ran to meet her - realising what a tremendous effort she had made to come the 100 miles by train, then bus, then a long walk on feet crippled with arthritis! I shall always look back on that as a Golden Day. Vicki was already much better, so we could relax and we talked and talked and just enjoyed being together - it was wonderful.

Within a year of Vicki's birth, Phil had applied for, and got a job at Hampton High School Melbourne, teaching Biology. We had a few regrets at leaving Bendigo, but they were far outweighed by our pleasure at the prospect at being back with our family and friends in Melbourne.

My father very kindly bought a house in the suburb of Middle Brighton (14 Heathfield Road) for us to live in. It was within easy reach of the sea, and during the hot summer months I got up early, rushed through the housework, and took the children down to the beach, potty chair, nappies and all! Phil would often join us there for a picnic lunch, as his school was fairly near.

Melbourne weather was famous for its unpredictability, and I well remember one day, before I was married, when the temperature dropped 40 degrees in half an hour! I had gone swimming in my lunch break from work, it was 95 degrees F. and during the time I was in the water and dressing, the wind had swung round to the South and the temperature dropped to 55 degrees F! However there were long periods of very hot weather when it was almost impossible to sleep at night. Very few homes had air-conditioning in those days.

As a little aside, I want to mention an incident that my mother described which will give you some idea of what a lovely little boy Laurie was. Mother was looking after Laurie and Vicki while Phil and I went into Melbourne to shop. Mother suffered badly from painful arthritis in her feet and hands, and she banged her foot and cried out. Laurie, aged 2 years, said "Ah! Marmar" with such love and concern and rushed across, dropped on the floor and kissed her hurting foot. That little incident was typical of Laurie's sensitivity and concern for other people. I managed to get Laurie into a local kindergarten for a few mornings a week, he loved it, though he was rather shy, and he got embarrassed easily. It made his day when Phil and I went along to his concerts and open days, but once he was satisfied that we were there, he never looked at us again until it was time to go home!

Those two years in Melbourne after we returned from Bendigo, were unsettled years. It was a strange feeling to be excluded from all the youthful activities at church, partly because of our family responsibilities, and partly by a deliberate decision of the youth group that no one over 22 years was welcome! That meant that I could go but Phil couldn't! There was no way I wanted to be there without Phil, but apart from that, we were upset for the many young single folk who were made to feel, old, rejected and past It. Phil was so incensed by this ruling, that he mentioned it in his next exhortation!

That caused no small stir, and from then on most of the young folk, and some of their parents gave us the cold shoulder.

Phil had developed into being a good public speaker, and on one occasion was asked to speak at a big Christadelphian gathering where the "Messiah" was being performed. He rather provocatively implied that Handel's music was far less significant than the work of the librettist who had selected the scriptures. Again, no small stir was created, and Phil was accused of getting too emotional about God.

Another unsettling feature of our experiences in the Melbourne Christadelphian world, was the awful bigotry and unloving attitudes which emerged when my father, bless him, who had always been a peace-maker, tried to help the divided Australian Christadelphians to reunite. Father travelled to all the major cities, visiting both sides, in an effort to get them talking to each other! I was with father and mother on some of these occasions and witnessed the tensions and violent emotions that many felt about the whole idea of reuniting with their Christadelphian brothers and sisters. You would have thought they were talking about out and out pagans, rather than fellow Christadelphians! In spite of this, after many many meetings large and small, much looking at scripture and a great deal of prayer, a reunion was achieved, largely through the dedication of my father and some loyal friends, mainly from England! Families that had been divided for over fifty years were brought together with tears and much rejoicing!

8 ENGLAND.

In trying to assess why we eventually felt we needed a break from Australia, it was an accumulation of negative factors within the Christadelphian world, a desire for Phil to see England, and the knowledge that with the two children still at pre-school age, it was now or possibly never! The final incentive to leave came with a rather strange incident. A combined choir from the Melbourne meetings met regularly to practise for several musical events each year. The standard of singing was good for an amateur choir, which numbered approximately fifty people. We got increasingly ambitious, and began hiring various Town Halls in which to perform, sometimes with choirs from other states. Someone then suggested that the women should all wear white and the men black for the performances. When my father heard of this suggestion, he made it known that he did not approve and saw it as a move to become more and more worldly! His attitude made him very unpopular, and if the Aussies go off you - you've had it! At the following choir practise I was accosted by an angry brother who laid into me about my father's attitude, he continued to harangue me even though I was in tears, and certainly not assuming any responsibility for my father's views, having been an independent married woman for five years! It took Phil quite a long time to comfort me when I got home that night.

It may seem a trivial thing on which to hang a decision to leave, but it was indicative of an attitude in Melbourne, which we could not feel comfortable with. Early in 1956 mother and father and Romie and Roger with Katy Julia and Elizabeth, decided to return to England permanently.

47

This has to be an added factor in the unsettling we felt. Father and mother painted a very rosy, and somewhat biased picture of the Old Country particularly to Phil, in an effort to persuade us also to return. I don't want to give the impression that we were coerced into our decision to leave, because we had already become excited at the thought of going to England, - the great adventure! Phil had hardly travelled in Australia, and he wanted to see England, as most Australians do. I won't bore you with the details of selling the house and furniture, (all having to be timed to coincide with our sailing date - Dec. 20 1956).

We stayed for the last couple of weeks with Phil's parents, it was so lovely to be with them. They had always been so kind and generous to the children, and us and we felt keenly for them as they faced the prospect of losing us to the other side of the world.

During that time, we were able to go twice to the Olympic Games, once with a school party, and once on our own. We saw Emil Zatterpeck, John Landy and Roger Banister (of four minute mile fame) - and then we saw the closing ceremony.

While we were at the Olympic Games, Phil's mum looked after Vicki and Laurie. She went in to wake Vicki up from her afternoon nap, only to find that she had unpopped all my dozens of strings of Poppet beads, and had them in a multi-coloured mountain on her lap! Mum said "What will your mummy say Vicki?" Vicki replied "Wash your step Vicki! Wash your step!"

December 20th arrived, hot and sunny, all final arrangements were complete, we now knew that we would not be going through the Suez Canal because of the Suez crisis, so our voyage would be via Durban and Cape Town, sailing North to the Canary Islands, through the Straits of Gibraltar, and along the English Channel to Tilbury. Our final meal was in Russell Collins Restaurant in the heart of Melbourne, with all the Hawkins family. The "Otranto" was scheduled to sail at 11pm, and we all drove down to Port Melbourne and everyone came to see our four berth cabin. There were lovely bunches of flowers everywhere, lots of hugs and kisses, and suppressed tears.

Phil's parents and sisters and families, had pockets full of coloured streamers which they threw to us from the quayside, and their faces were lit up by the twinkling harbour lights. The dozens of streamers, our last link with the land, got longer and longer and then broke one by one as 'Otranto' set sail. (The image of that farewell is indelibly etched on our minds). By this time, it was nearly midnight, we were well out into Port Philip Bay, and the children were exhausted. We soon got them into their bunks, Laurie on the top and Vicki below. We had deliberately not mentioned anything about the possibility of sea-sickness, so when in the early hours of the morning, the ship moved out of Port Philip Bay into the notorious waters of the Great Australian Bight and the deck below us started to heave, we knew that Laurie meant it when he said as his feet touched the deck "I feel sick!" With those words commenced a period of intense internal upheaval for Laurie Phil and me! Vicki remained totally unaffected and ravenously hungry for the whole voyage! Seasickness has to be one of the worst physical experiences possible to mankind. I will not dwell on it, except to comment that on arrival at Adelaide, and a whole day ashore with friends, the mere sight of the ship as we drove towards it at the end of the day, was enough to bring on the nausea again! We spent Christmas day with dear friends in Perth, and we were gradually getting our sea legs, as we waved goodbye to the sandy beaches and lovely sunshine of Western Australia. For eleven days crossing the Indian Ocean we were out of the sight of land, (the nearest being the land below us!). As we neared Durban it became very rough, amazing to see a huge liner being thrown around like a child's toy! but by now we had our 'sea-legs' and were enjoying the exhilaration of sea travel.

Laurie and Vicki spent much of the day in the children's play area, and they had their evening meal earlier than us, so when later in the voyage, there was a fancy dress party for the kids as we crossed the equator, and Laurie and Vicki won the second prize as a King and Queen dressed in crepe paper, people asked us whose children they were, and were amazed to find out that they were ours! (They had all thought we were on our honeymoon!) By the time we had our evening meal the children were in bed, at least that was the theory! Many a time we looked up to the deck above to see two little faces peering through the carved screen which surrounded the dining room, then racing off to the cabin when we looked! Vicki took to spending ages in the bathroom soaping her hands and arms, then dashing to the cabin white nighty and blue ribbons flying! Breakfast time became something of a challenge - we ate at a table with two other families, and Vicki sensed that she could get away with murder as she surmised we wouldn't tell her off in front of others!

Things got progressively worse each day as she mucked about with her food and generally misbehaved. I warned her that if she tried it on next morning she would have a smacked bottom! Breakfast time arrived and Vicki got up to her tricks again. I picked her up and strode out to the women's toilets. She knew "judgement day" had come and ended up with a very pink rear end. In the midst of this, a male steward stormed into the washroom and told me I was a wicked mother and she would grow up to hate me just as he hated his mother. I told him to mind his own business and get out! I should add that pretty 'angelic' little Vicki was the darling of all the stewards on the ship.

We spent a very interesting time in Durban and visited a native Kraal. Vicki says she can still remember the smell of it to this day! The Cape of Good Hope lived up to its reputation as one of the roughest oceans in the world. Next we reached Cape Town, such a beautiful city, with that amazing Table Mountain always dominating the scene. We decided to share a taxi with another family for the day, and were taken to all the famous sights in and around Cape Town. We had an Afrikaans driver, and we were appalled at his racism - swearing at the blacks with such hatred as he drove us around. We were continually brought face to face with apartheid, bus stops - whites only, swimming pools - no blacks allowed etc. etc.. It made us so glad we did not live there.

After a second day in Cape Town, we set sail for the Canary Islands, and had the long haul north up the West Coast of Africa. S.S.Otranto had seen better days, in fact she had been a troop ship in the second world war! There had been a re-fit since then, but she was not the most luxurious vessel afloat! Because our voyage had been diverted around the Cape due to the Suez crisis, we were longer at sea than expected, and the drinking water was running out! We noticed oil floating on the drinking water at dinner, and asked the steward about it. He explained that they had had to resort to the emergency tank, which had previously contained fuel oil! The Captain then informed us that instead of the scheduled stop at Las Palmas, we would have to call in at Dakar in French West Africa for fresh water supplies. This proved to be a fascinating place, not used to tourists, therefore far more natural, and truly African. (Little did we realise then, that our two year old daughter who Phil carried on his shoulders in Dakar, would one day be living on this same continent, or that our granddaughter Laura would be born in a primitive Mission Hospital in Cameroon!).

Excitement increased on board the Otranto, as we came through the Bay of Biscay and round into the English Channel. It was late January, cold, windy, and the sea was rough. Gone were the tropical white uniforms of the ship's officers, the reality of the Northern Hemisphere climate was upon us! Laurie celebrated his fifth birthday on board ship on January 12th, so hard to believe he was now school age. Vicki was three the day before we docked at Tilbury. As we tied up, we searched the shore for familiar faces, and saw mother and father waving ecstatically! We were in cold grey uninviting England. No leaves on the trees, no colour, just grey drizzle.

When at last spring arrived, we were in Worthing staying with my parents. I vividly remember the day Phil and I took a ride on a double-decker bus out into the country, we just could not get over the beauty of the English countryside in spring. We were amazed that people in the bus were not all staring out of the window and gasping at the view instead of reading their newspapers!

The quicker I pass over the first few months in England the better! We had sold up everything in order to pay the £500 for our fares. Phil had no job and it was in the middle of the school year, (not a good time to get one,) we had no home and no money! There were several occasions during those first six months when we wondered what on earth we had done, leaving beautiful sunny Australia with its lovely houses and glorious beaches, to come to miserable unfriendly England. Phil got a temporary job in Bristol, filling in for a teacher who had had a nervous breakdown! All the stories of the marvellous British Education System crumbled to ashes as Phil experienced the challenges of Kingswood Grammar School. If it hadn't been for the love and compassion of my dear sister Romie, I don't know how I would have survived those months in Bristol. She welcomed me day after day when I landed on her doorstep because I was depressed and lonely. Poor little Laurie had a bad start at Ashley Down School with a harsh teacher who had no sympathy for his bewilderment and tears.

But worst of all was our encounter with the Bristol Cheltenham Road Christadelphian Church! We arrived on Sunday morning, and took our seats near the back of this one time cinema. We smiled at the folks around us, only to be met by stern faced stares from every direction! Not a glimmer of friendliness or welcome. After the service, nobody came up to us, and when we attempted to approach people, they either ignored us or quickly turned back to their conversations with their friends. The one redeeming feature was that eventually an elderly couple called Yearsley made their way to the back, and sought us out, they had known Phil's father many years before and were delighted to find that this was his son and family. We visited their home several times after that, and grew very fond of them.

It was a beautiful summer that year, 1957, and our flat in Westbury Park was near the Downs, so we spent a lot of time out in the hot sun playing with the children and having picnics. The flat itself was in a posh area, but was pretty basic. We had to pay six months' rent in advance for it, how naive can you get?! Below us were several men who seemed to own the whole house, (we suspected they were gay), and sometimes they would get drunk and break the lock on the dividing door to our flat, it was quite scary. We were ready for a move.

9 CRAWLEY

Phil knew that the Kingswood Grammar School post was only temporary thankfully, so he applied for a job in Crawley New Town in West Sussex. He was called for interview, and when he arrived back in Bristol that evening I was thrilled to hear that he had been appointed Head of Biology at Ifield Grammar School. Another positive thing was that a house went with the job! So during the summer holidays we moved to a brand-new house in a half completed district of Crawley called Tilgate. It was so good to be able to unpack the things we had brought with us from Australia, our wedding presents and small treasures that we had not seen since we left Melbourne! Laurie started at the Desmond Anderson School, just down the road, and he settled in quickly. Everything was fresh and new in Crawley, with bright coloured doors on the houses, and lots of green grass and trees. Tilgate was still being built, even the houses next to us were not finished. The shopping precinct was still an architect's dream, and we had to buy essentials from a mobile shop parked near where the shops

would be! There were Alsatian guard dogs patrolling around the streets near us to prevent theft of building materials. Like most new towns, Crawley was built to take people from overcrowded parts of London.

Phil and I were starting to feel more settled and much happier with our decision to come to England. We joined the Crawley Christadelphians, and were made very welcome, we grew to love those people a lot, and we took a very active part in the church life. Phil, Laurie and Vicki, saw their first snow at the end of the year, and had great fun building a snowman in our small front garden. One of my precious memories, is the day of Laurie's school fete. He went off to school with a small amount of pocket money, and came back home with an ornament, which held bought off the bric-a-brac stall for me. I can still see him proudly carrying it home, he had thought of me when he could so easily have spent it on himself. On another occasion, Laurie turned up at home at lunchtime, thinking it was the end of the day, much to his horror and consternation! He was like his dad, a bit of a dreamer!

One day I was surprised to get a message from Laurie's Headmistress at Bishop Bell School, asking me to go and see her. I wondered what on earth was wrong, only to discover that she was concerned about Laurie's lack of progress at school. They had given him an I.Q. test and found he was above average, therefore they could not understand why he was not answering them in class, and not progressing with his work, especially reading. At first she thought he was just being awkward in not responding to them, then she suspected that his hearing was defective. We were shocked to have our own suspicions confirmed, and arranged to have his hearing tested. This involved several visits to the Ears Nose and Throat Hospital in London. His hearing was far from perfect, and the consultant said he needed his tonsils and adenoids out as soon as possible. Some of the tests he had to undergo were very painful, poor lad, so I always tried to give him a treat afterwards to compensate for what he had been through. This would sometimes be a visit to the News Theatre on Victoria Station, with an hour-long programme of mostly cartoons, which we both loved. (Remember we had no TV in those days.)

We booked Laurie into Crawley Hospital to have his tonsils out, and when he came home after the operation, we couldn't believe the difference in his breathing at night, it was so quiet that we had to go up close to him to make sure he was still alive! The improvement in his hearing was dramatic, so we never regretted the decision to have the operation done despite dire warnings from my parents that he might die during the operation! My father had never got over the shock of having his own tonsils out, without anaesthetic, on the kitchen table in 1904! In spite of all this, Laurie's reading progress was almost non-existent Phil spent many hours with him patiently trying everything he could think of to help Laurie have a breakthrough, nothing seemed to work, until one day when Laurie was nearly nine years old it all fell into place! He then became an avid reader, devouring anything he could get his hands on, including some really "heavy" literature like 'Masterman Ready' and "Treasure Island." Of course this late start had held Laurie up in other subjects as well, so when it came round to the much vaunted 11+ exam, Laurie failed but was allotted a place at Britain's newest and biggest Comprehensive School - Thomas Bennett. We had asked that he could go to Sarah Robinson School, a Secondary Modern School next door to Phil's Ifield Grammar, because we felt a good Secondary Modern would be better for him than a massive comprehensive school, where he might be swallowed up and lose his enthusiasm. We had to appeal several times to get Laurie into Sarah Robinson, but eventually we won! Within a year he was top of his class and was transferred to the Grammar School. He never looked back from then on.

Meanwhile, how about Vicki? As indicated by the aforementioned escapades on board ship, she was no more perfect than the rest of us, however she was always a great source of joy to Phil and me. I can honestly say that I have never known Vicki say an unkind or cruel thing in her life. She was a happy and carefree child, and particularly after Laurie went to school, a great companion to me. We had so much fun together, reading stories, doing interesting table activities, cooking, learning words and numbers, playing with water, and painting etc.

I can still see her cycling round and round the plot of grass in front of our house in Tilgate, on her second hand tricycle! Later It was roller skates that, were the craze. She was a 'natural' at all kinds of sport from an early age.

I dreaded the day when she was to start school - the end of such a precious era. She looked so smart in her Bishop Bell uniform of a bright red blazer and grey skirt. She was very excited and I knew she would soon settle in with Laurie to look after her. (They were very close and good friends, they rarely quarrelled, our main challenge was trying to get them to stop them giggling and larking about when it was time for bed!) I met the children at lunchtime, and Vicki was full of everything she had done at school. Her only complaint was that Miss Mitten her teacher kept shouting. Vicki could just about read when she started school, so her progress was rapid, which only tended to emphasise the difficulty Laurie was having, we felt for him so much.

Vicki's bubbling energy sometimes led her into trouble. Unbeknown to us, she had discovered she could jump out of our first floor bedroom window onto the lawn! So guess what? She dared Laurie to do the same! We were sitting in the dining room, when we heard a scuffling noise in the front entrance hall. We found Laurie lying there in a lot of pain, the story was that he had jumped down the stairs and hurt his leg. Later we learned the truth! I'm afraid we did not take his hurting leg seriously enough, and he hobbled around for days on what turned out to be a broken leg! (So sorry Laurie) Laurie soon adapted to his plaster and crutches, and went leaping along to school at the rate of knots and became quite a hero! Laurie was 10 and Vicki 8 when this happened, and it coincided with an exciting visit of Phil's parents from Australia; but more of that later.

A little glimpse into Vicki's personality will be seen in the following episode. She was about seven years old and she knocked her hand which hurt her badly enough to bring tears. Sometime later, I went up to kiss her goodnight and found her crying. My immediate thought was to ask her if her hand still hurt, but she answered "No mummy, I was just imagining what it must have been like for Jesus when they hammered the nails into his hands". This was no put on sentimentality; it was a seven year old little girl entering the feelings of Jesus who she loved with all her heart. Those moments are so precious when parents see a spontaneous response to spiritual things in their children.

As I write, I realise that I am describing life very much from my viewpoint, and what I did and said - understandable in an autobiography I suppose, but I must insert here some comments about my beloved Phil and the immense source of encouragement and love he was, and is, to all of us. Phil played a vital part in all the events I have been attempting to describe so far. His rock-like strength and faith, were always there to lean on and be comforted by. If any of us felt down or unwell, we always experienced reassurance and empathy from him. Our love for each other grew and deepened with every year that passed. In all the essentials we saw things the same way. Above all, our growth as followers of Jesus went side by side. our searching questions about God, life, religion, the world, gave us many hours of stimulating discussion together. Phil's involvement with Laurie and Vicki (and later Jamie) was total. He never had to be asked twice to play with them - no matter how engrossed he was with his own work or studies, their needs were always a priority. It was not a chore, but a source of joy to him, and their growth as children of God was far more important than academic achievements. When they brought their reports home with high or low marks, the first thing we looked at were the comments of staff about the way they interacted with other people and life in general. Not that we discounted academic achievements, we were just as thrilled as they were when they did well, but the message we tried to give them, was that we loved them unconditionally.

One of the great bonuses of being married to a school teacher, was the school holidays. We so looked forward to having the children home and doing things together. We could not run to expensive holidays, so we went camping! I had my first experience of camping in Australia, and I have to admit I was not a 'natural' when it came to living under canvas, even in that climate. As for camping in England, squelching across sodden fields to primitive toilets, cowering in the tent through thunder storms, seeing the butter turn to oil and the milk go bad when the sun did shine, and finding crawling creatures in the sleeping bags, well that's not my idea of fun! However Phil, who is the real adventurer, persuaded me to join him and the kids for some fantastic holidays on the continent.

One year we spent six weeks travelling all over France, and we only had one day of rain! We saw Paris, Orange, Nimes, The Pont du Gard, Nice, Toulouse, Toulon, Mentone, and Monte Carlo, and we got as far as the Spanish border, we even crossed the Alps! All this was achieved in our old Bradford Jowett van packed to the roof with camping gear.

People just could not believe that a vehicle that appeared so ancient, could actually run, and at one place a man with a huge grin on his face, standing outside a car scrap yard, beckoned us in, I could have slapped him!

On our journey home, first we had a scare, then a catastrophe! Driving through a small cobbled-stoned French town, we suddenly heard a clanking sound coming from the rear of the Bradford, our hearts in our mouths, we stopped and discovered that one of the children's metal spades had fallen through a gap in the floor boards and was banging on the road! Not long after that there was a loud bang, and the car shuddered to a halt, Phil's face was a picture, he knew - this was serious! It turned out that the main leaf spring at the rear of the car had broken in two! Here we were in a foreign country, unable to speak French (except my stumbling attempts dredged up from my school days) with a car packed to the roof with heavy camping gear, and a husband sweating with anxiety! We limped our way to La Charité-sur-Loire, and a favourite campsite on the banks of the Loire. Phil's brain had been working overtime as to a possible solution, which would save us from massive repair bills. He came up with a brainwave - two steel plates with a bolt at each corner to clamp the offending spring together. The challenge now was to find someone to make the steel plates who could understand 'sign language'. The children and I enjoyed the pleasures of swimming in the river and fun and games, while poor Phil tackled the task of mending the car. At last we repacked the car, and held our breath as we cautiously made our way to Calais, and then reminded ourselves to drive on the left to Crawley! That steel plate remained on the car until we sold it and bought a Ford Anglia in 1962!

10 A NEW DIRECTION.

Early in our life in Crawley, about 1960, we had an experience which changed the direction of our lives!

For some time we had known a man called Sidney Clementson, he came to preach at Crawley meeting, and to be brutally frank we found him somewhat boring, and slightly irritating in his mannerisms. When we heard he was coming to our Bible class to give six talks on the book of Revelation, we both groaned and prepared to be even more switched off the subject than we had been in Melbourne! Those talks were like a shaft of light into our hearts, and Sidney and his wife Elizabeth, though old enough to be our parents, became two of our dearest friends. Sidney's opening words were "My dear brothers and sisters all you need to understand the book of Revelation is your Bible." He then proceeded to illustrate from scripture what he meant - that we did not need to read other people's expositions on the Revelation, the clues were all there in scripture for anyone to search out. Even the humblest most uneducated person whose heart's desire was to know more about Jesus' last message, could do so with God's help. Sidney had kindled in us a burning desire to know more, he had set us on a road which one day would lead us inevitably out of our narrow Christadelphian world. Bible study became exciting and challenging, it was as if we were on a treasure hunt. Whole sections of scripture that had been meaningless or irrelevant or beyond our reach, started to open up before us. Instead of studying Revelation to acquire Knowledge and seem clever, we found we were being challenged to examine our relationship with Jesus. We had never thought like that before! Could he really want a personal relationship with us? It blew our minds! We started to look at the rest of scripture as if with eyes that had just been healed of blindness. Professors Whitcomb and Morris challenged our attitude to Genesis, which had been somewhat ambivalent, in their amazing book "The Genesis Flood". Their message was go back to Genesis and read it with the trust and simplicity of a child, uncluttered by preconceived ideas, and start listening to the one who was there, and not to the compromises of the world around us. Phil, as a trained Biologist, had been subtly influenced by the thinking of the evolutionists, and as a Christian tried to fit Genesis around the theories of science. Instead, we were learning that having the receptivity of children, did not mean closing our eyes to the findings of science and burying our heads in the sand, but looking at the world around us in the light of what God has told us first! From Genesis to the writings of Paul John and Peter, the age of the Holy Spirit is the age we are living in! We had been brought up to believe that the Holy Spirit was used to establish the church, and then had been withdrawn - so any scripture that suggested that He - the Holy Spirit was available to the believer, was talking about first century Christians only. What a tragedy we had been caught up in - "a form of religion denying the power thereof". So the stone that Sidney had started rolling in our lives was gathering momentum, and in God's wise and gracious way, He little by little, opened our eyes to the fundamental doctrines of the true Gospel.

Back to family matters, when Laurie was 10 and Vicki 8 years old, Phil and I felt the urge to return to live in Australia. So, we wrote to Phil's parents telling them of our plans. We received a letter by return of post, saying that they had booked their passages on the ship Johann Van Oldenbarnavelt to come to England for nine months, so please would we postpone our return! With great joy we welcomed Mum and Dad, and they stayed with us all the time between their trips around the country, visiting old friends and familiar places.

Phil's Mum had left England with her father and brothers and sisters when she was sixteen, and Dad was born in Sydney, a third generation Aussie. I am so grateful that Laurie and Vicki had the opportunity to get to know their grandparents in those months, I'm only sorry that Jamie never knew them. The happy time slipped by, and the day came when we drove them down to Southampton to sail back on the J.V.0. We had the sad conviction that we would never see them again. Mum had already had a stroke, and Dad was over 80 years old. Within two years they were both dead, along with Stuart, Phil's brother-in-law, who died in a car accident, leaving Marty and three children penniless, (even though he was an insurance agent!). All three died within a few weeks of each other - it was like a nightmare as one cablegram followed another. Our return trip to Australia was cancelled, and Phil started doing research for a PhD at London University, and our busy life in Crawley continued. A little cameo of Laurie as a young boy in Crawley Meeting. We had encouraged him to take notes of the talks (partly to stave off boredom!) and he nearly always did, but he also took in what was being said to the extent that after the service he sometimes went up and discussed the talk with the speakers, much to their amazement.

When Phil's parents had returned to Australia and of course the children were out all day at school, I began to feel more and more in need of some occupation outside the home. I longed to fulfil my ambition to be a teacher, which had been thwarted by going into my parent's business so many years before, applied, and was called for an interview at Bishop Otter College in Chichester. I did very well at the first round, the vice-Principal quizzed me for ages, and indicated how pleased she was with how I responded. Then she passed me on to a male member of staff who homed in on my desire to do theology as my main subject. He proceeded to challenge my stance as a Christian saying "You may come here with some Christian beliefs, but I can assure you that when you leave it will be a different story!" He was extremely aggressive and provocative, and I rose to the bait! I said "I'm fully prepared to review and rethink my theological ideas and concepts, but there are certain basic truths that I am not likely to change". "What are they?" he asked. "The belief that Jesus Christ rose from the dead and is my Saviour" I answered. I knew that as far as he was concerned, I had blown it. He was not prepared to have such a bigoted Christian in his college! I was disappointed in one way, but in another, I was relieved. It would have meant travelling to Chichester each day and having less and less time with Phil and the children. Once more my longing to be involved in teaching was deferred.

Shortly after that, the headmistress of the children's school - Bishop Bell, asked me if I would like to be a dinner lady. (Meal Supervisor being the official title!). I was delighted, it meant getting to school at 12 noon, looking after the children (including Vicki) in the playground (or inside on rainy days) during the lunch hour, then having a meal with the kitchen staff. The money came in handy too! That job lasted for four years until one day a friend at school pointed out an advertisement in the local paper for someone to work in a playgroup run by the NSPCC I applied and got the Job and my life started to move in a new direction. I little realised that a door had opened which would lead me into one of the most fulfilling occupations of my life.

But I jump ahead! Several years before this, Phil and I discussed the possibility of having a baby! Laurie and Vicki were born when we were very young and we had always had at the back of our minds the thought of another family in our "old ages". I was coming up to 34 years old and we decided it was now or never! To our delight I conceived the next month! By this time, Laurie was nearly 14 years old and over 6 foot tall, and Vicki was 12 years. They still used to come into our bed for an early morning cuppa each day! One morning we decided to break the news, so Phil said "Hey kids we've got some news for you" - they looked up curiously, and Phil said "Mum

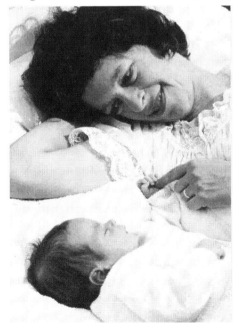

is expecting a baby" - there was a deathly hush, then Vicki said "Oh go on Dad" she clearly did not believe us. I then confirmed, that what Phil had said was true! It sunk in at last, and Vicki nearly exploded with excitement and joy. Meanwhile Laurie lay in total silence taking the news in his way. It must have been really strange for them to get used to the thought that after all these years they were going to have a little sister or brother! My pregnancy went well, in fact people told me that I looked ten years younger!

This time we decided to have the birth at home, and at last Phil would be able to be present. There was a lovely midwife living opposite, so we could call her day or night. Labour started early on the very day that the baby was officially due, December 9th. I did the last minute shopping, drew out some money, washed my hair, and cleaned the house! Laurie and Vicki were each wanting a baby of their own sex, and were jokingly vying with each other about the outcome. The interval between the contractions was down to five minutes, and the pain increased dramatically. This continued all day, but at last we went to bed and tried to get some sleep, but in the middle of the night we realised that things were not as they should be. Phil ran across the road to fetch the midwife, and when she saw me, she immediately phoned the Doctor. He found that I had moved into a late stage of labour, but the baby's head was not able to get through the tight neck of my womb (just like with Laurie's birth). The Doctor phoned for an ambulance, and our dream of a home delivery went for ever. I shall never forget that dash through the streets of Crawley - the siren shattering the quiet night as I practically ate the gas and air machine in an attempt to get some relief from the intense pain. Phil sat by me in the labour ward, at least he was with me for the birth this time! However even that longing was to be thwarted! The Norwegian doctor kept listening to the baby's heartbeat and ever increasing signs of stress. Forms were brought in to sign for a Caesarean Section to be done immediately. Phil was asked to wait outside after he'd signed the form. Then the doctor, who was a lovely gentle and kind man, said he would try one more time to bring the baby naturally. He drained my bladder - agony! Then he pushed with all his strength the neck of my womb with his rubber gloved fingers, and at last released the poor little head of our darling son Jamie from that wretched prison. I looked and saw him hanging upside down - his feet in the doctor's hand - he was yelling his head off and he was alive! (During that protracted labour, there was grave concern for Jamie's life, and also for mine).

I hope Jim, as you read this you will understand why I could not face going through all this again, so you were destined to be like an only child - but oh what a blessing to our lives you have been. Romie came to look after me for a few days, which was lovely, little Jamie smiled at her when he was only two days old! Both Laurie and Vicki were absolutely wonderful with Jamie.

Vicki would proudly walk down the street with the pram, and show him off to her friends. She helped me bath him, and was like another mother to him in many ways. Laurie was a kind big brother who was always good fun and he and Jamie had many a laugh.

I shall always remember the day I came home from hospital with Jamie, he was only two days old and it was a cold day in December. Phil had put an electric fire in the bedroom. There were masses of flowers from family and friends, and the treasure cot with its frills and lace was by my bed. A roast dinner was cooking in the oven, and Phil, Laurie, and Vicki were there to welcome us both - it was so wonderful to be home.

My mother got tremendous pleasure from Jamie the baby of the family, they had a wonderful relationship, I only regret that Jamie cannot remember his lovely grandmother.

Laurie was about 14 years of age, when the music teacher came up to Phil at school and said "Are you on good terms with your neighbours?" Phil said "Yes, why?" He answered "Would you still be on good terms if he learns to play the bass trombone?" So began an exciting new interest in Laurie's life which firstly led to the school orchestra, and then the County Youth Orchestra, with trips at home and abroad. We actually grew to love the mellow tones of his trombone as he practised up in his bedroom. Laurie played in numerous concerts, and I remember taking two year-old Jamie to his first concert when Laurie was playing at Ifield school. We were sitting quite near the back, but Jamie was eager to see his big brother playing, and was so fascinated by the music that he stood on a chair and never moved nor took his eyes off the orchestra for the whole performance! We still regret not letting Laurie buy a 12 string guitar that he was offered and which he would have loved to play, looking back I cannot understand what our thinking was, but we are so sorry Laurie, please forgive us!

In 1965 Vicki passed the 11+ and was one of the last intake to Ifield Grammar School before it became a 14 form entry Comprehensive School! So now, Phil had both his children keeping an eye on him, or vice versa, at school! I remember Vicki saying at breakfast one day "Dad, do you realise how many times you said "I want to make it abundantly clear" in assembly yesterday?" We often had a laugh over the children's feedback about their dad! It worked the other way too, sometimes teachers would 'tell tales' about

Laurie and Vicki, which annoyed Phil immensely. (He thought they should deal with our children as they would with any other students). Phil also knew too much about their peers to allow them to go to certain parties, which must have been most irritating for them. In the sixties, Crawley was in the national news as a place with a huge drugs problem.

Our children had many tough challenges at this time, some we know about, and many of which we don't. We thank God that they came through the worst excesses of temptations and both had the character to be 'their own person' and the will to act on their deep down desire to please God. It was not an easy time for them, we were strict and at times unreasonable I'm sure, but neither was it easy for us, as any parent of teenagers knows! Having been so close to Vicki as a little girl, we suddenly seemed to be living with a stranger. Our quiet and sensitive daughter had become a gum chewing, cigarette smoking, mini-skirted young woman, who didn't seem to like us much. She was never noisily rebellious or aggressively disobedient, but a lot was going on that gave us pain and made us wonder how we had gone wrong?

(I remember Vicki saying years later, if ever you come across my diaries written in my teens, destroy them, don't read them, which helps you to imagine her feelings in those difficult days). Meanwhile Laurie had to come to terms with a bad case of acne which no amount of washing, dieting, and treatments seemed to help. Our hearts went out to him, particularly when he suffered the after effects of the sun-ray treatment which almost brought him to tears. It was a great challenge to him and he was brave and uncomplaining.

On a much happier note, I shall never forget one day when Laurie, aged 14, was talking to me in the kitchen and with tears in his eyes expressed the desire to commit his life to Christ. It was a highly significant decision in his life and one that he felt deeply and sincerely. It meant more to us than any of his other achievements, and later on he expressed the view that his baptism and commitment at that relatively young age, acted as an anchor to him as he faced the decisions and temptations of teenage years and university life. As in my own life - (baptised at 15 years of age) in spite of the Christadelphian environment, misguided concepts and wrong doctrines, Laurie's decision was to do with a response to Jesus, not a desire to join a religious group.

In the course of the next few years, Laurie and Vicki went off the Christadelphian meetings, and came along reluctantly or simply refused to come at all. One evening meeting when they did come, Vicki was wearing a cape that I had made for her, and with her long hair it was easy to conceal the wire from her earplug connected to her hidden radio as she listened to "Top of the Pops." Phil and I quite understood how they felt as we were often bored stiff as well. In fact, we were feeling less and less comfortable with the whole Christadelphian set up. I well remember one evening meeting at Crawley, when Phil had given a talk about the book of Revelation, and had dared to express views that were different from the usual Christadelphian line. Afterwards a man went up to Phil and with some anger said "Are you implying that you know better than our founder Dr. Thomas?" This sort of thing happened over and over again as we shared with people the discoveries we were making about the books of Daniel and Revelation, since our eyes had been opened by Sidney Clementson. We were also being challenged in our thinking on scripture in general, and it was like a new conversion - a sense of being born again! We read scriptures that we had known all our lives and they suddenly came to life. We realised that the wonderful and inspiring words that Jesus and Paul wrote to the early Christians could also apply to us in these days. We started to eagerly examine the numerous references to the Holy Spirit and long for His transforming power and influence in our lives.

In 1968 Phil was asked to become Science Editor of the Christadelphian 'Testimony' magazine. This involved writing about the wonders of creation, and he produced some fascinating articles. Every month the manuscript for the whole magazine landed on our doormat, and together we read through all the writers contributions. (If two sub-editors objected to anything, it would not be printed!). It was as a result of Phil's articles in the 'Testimony' that he was invited to speak at some seminars in Canada in 1969, and that opened up a whole new world!

After 7 years working for the Testimony, an issue arose that brought Phil to a moment of personal challenge, and led to his resignation. Most of the Testimony committee wanted to publish an article, which condemned the beliefs of a very well known Christadelphian preacher, called Alfred Norris. Alfred was 'daring' to publish articles and books about the work of the Holy Spirit in our lives today, with which the traditionalists did not agree, they considered it heresy, however Phil and I were of one mind with Alfred Norris and could not join in with such public condemnation. Phil was the only dissenter on the committee, and when they said they would publish anyway, he handed in his resignation. This cost Phil dearly because he had invested so much of himself in the work for the Testimony. I remember vividly him arriving home that evening, and when he told me what had happened, he broke down. Most of all he was deeply grieved because of the blindness that could cause Bible readers to reject the truth that the Holy Spirit is available and essential for Christians today.

Meanwhile Laurie and Vicki were moving into the serious business of O and A levels, and Jamie was emerging as a 'character' in his own right! He had a strong will, and I remember at the end of a particularly trying day when Phil came home from school, I said "I think I'm losing the battle with Jamie!" Phil encouraged me and said "Hey come on - are you going to let a little lad of two years old get the better of you? Just be firm with him for a couple of weeks, and I'm sure he will respond." So I braced myself and put a note of determination into my voice, tried to be consistent and sound as though I meant what I was saying, and after a couple of weeks, I asked Jamie to do something, and he immediately obeyed me. When Phil got home, I said, "I think I've won the battle!" From then on, Jamie and I got on like a house on fire!

It was about that time that by accident, Jamie started to read! He found a card with Vicki's name written on it, brought it to me and asked what it said. A few days later he found the card again, came to me and said "Vicki". I was surprised that he had remembered, and I wondered if he would be able to memorise other words, so I copied out, the sixteen words from the first Ladybird reading book onto flash cards. Within a week Jamie knew all sixteen words, and he then proceeded to read through the book itself! By the time he was two years old he had read the first three Ladybird reading books! (I can't help wondering how many other children would do the same, given the opportunity!). Jamie and I always had a 'special' time together in the afternoon when we would play learning games, reading, counting buttons and sorting them into piles of the same colour etc. I always felt it should be fun, and resisted putting pressure on him if he did not feel in the mood, or showing him off to people. Because of this early stimulation, Jamie became an avid reader, and was ready for school well before he was 5 years old. Reflecting on this has brought to mind my own mother, I'm so grateful that I had such a lovely mother, full of life and enthusiasm, able to convey to me as a very young child, how much God loved me, and the excitement of knowing Jesus. She always made me feel loved and valued, something I probably took for granted, but now realise that many do not have that assurance, and it is so precious. During the time that mother lived with us in Crawley after her accident, we had some wonderful talks that I shall always treasure in my mind.

When Jamie was 4, Vicki 16, and Laurie 18 years old, and shortly to leave for University in Manchester, I became more and more conscious of a whacking big void in my own life, and I was very lonely. Although I enjoyed homemaking and bringing up the children, I suspected that there were other things in life as well! I longed to be someone in my own right, to use my skills, to be fulfilled and busy. I had been working part time at Bishop Bell School, looking after the children in the lunch hour, and I little realised that through a casual remark made by my friend Marg Kelvie, a whole new dimension was about to open in my life. I was round at Marg's house after school having a cup of tea, when she said "Have you seen the advert in the paper for someone to work for the NSPCC? We didn't even get that paper, so I would never have known about it unless Marg had mentioned it. I applied and got the job!

I believe this was a real answer to prayer, from that moment I had a sense of fulfilment and of being prepared for so much that was to follow in our lives. My contact with both the parents and children, opened my eyes to a world that I hardly knew existed, (from my sheltered and protected Christadelphian environment). I saw children who were blind, deaf, and paralysed, as a result of being battered by their parents. I saw many children who did not know how to smile, let alone laugh, because they were so unhappy. I also saw large families living in squalor, who had to be moved out of their houses periodically, so that the filth could be scraped off the floor and walls, and everything disinfected! I heard of cohabiting set ups that blew my mind, and eventually I found that there was not much that could shock me! I grew to love those poor deprived and mistreated children so much, my heart ached for them. Occasionally I had the opportunity to talk to them about God, and at Christmas, I was allowed to organise a nativity play, but my boss who was very much into 'New Age' philosophy frowned on my overt Christianity. Gradually a longing took seed in my heart, that one day I would be able to run my own Christ-centred Playgroup, so bringing in the missing ingredient that was vital, more of that later!

In 1967, my dear mother had an accident in her bedroom, she turned awkwardly and fell down and broke her femur. She was taken into Weston-Super-Mare Hospital and the shock and the pain from the accident nearly killed her. Had nature been left to take its course I think she would have died then, however modern drugs and treatments brought her round and gave her two more years of life, but life filled with agony and the indignity of total incontinence and dependency. She had to be lifted by a hoist, she never regained her ability to walk, and so she lived in a wheel chair. We saw our lovely vibrant mother gradually decline into rapid old age and senility, even losing some of her mental powers. I had the privilege of caring for her for several months to give father a break, and I am eternally grateful for that precious time together. During mother's two years of suffering, I developed some troublesome symptoms, which I suppose would be described as 'panic attacks'. Palpitations, sleeplessness, anxiety and constant worry about mother. On April 23 1969, the phone rang and Romie, who had been with her constantly for the last few days, and off and on for weeks, and was there at the end, told us that our darling was dead. The funeral was a difficult time of course for all of us. I refused to see mother's body beforehand - something I now deeply regret, and I went into a period of denial for about six months, followed by delayed reaction which led to deep depression for several frightening weeks.

Phil's love, reassurance, prayers and supreme patience, brought me through, and I can even, from this point in time, be grateful for the experience, because it helps me to have genuine empathy for depressed people who come for counselling

.

11 LEAVING THE NEST

The time had come for Laurie to leave home.   He had done very well in his 'A' level Maths, Physics, and Chemistry, and after several attempts, had even passed his 'O' level English! Manchester was his chosen University, and we all went up to see him settled in and say goodbye.   Vicki was chafing at the bit to be free of home restraints and envied her brother very much! Laurie's leaving home left a huge gap in our lives - we missed him so much and eagerly looked forward to the occasional phone call or letter home.   Phil had difficulty in coming to terms with the ever increasing length of Laurie's hair each time he came home on holiday, and I'm afraid gave him a hard time, something Phil regretted very much later and asked Laurie's forgiveness, duly received!

In the interval between Laurie's departure to Manchester and Vicki also leaving home, Jamie started at Furnace Green School a year ahead of his age group.   Fortunately he had a teacher who was sympathetic to his particular needs, as she discovered that he already had a reading age of about 9 or 10, (not all teachers were happy with parents who taught their children at home!). At this time, we were trying more and more desperately to leave Crawley. Phil applied for several Jobs and was called for interviews but nothing came of them.   It wasn't as though we did not love the brothers and sisters in Crawley Christadelphian Church, but we were feeling that we needed the stimulation of fresh ideas and challenges, and the fellowship of a wider circle of Christian friends.   Above all we were becoming more and more uncomfortable with the Christadelphian context, bit by bit, doctrine by doctrine, God was opening our minds and hearts to fresh insights and truths. We were hungry and thirsty for more of Jesus and the Holy Spirit in our lives, in other words a Living Faith!

As I mentioned a few pages back, Phil's work on the Testimony Magazine led to Ted Farrar of Hamilton Ontario Canada, inviting Phil to speak at a Bible and Science Seminar he had organised at McMaster University in Hamilton. He had also arranged for radio and T.V. appearances interviews and phone-in programmes. It was to be a ten-day tour, and we could not afford a ticket for me as well, but at the last moment someone we hardly knew, paid for me to go with Phil! Wow! What an amazing time that was!

The Bible Science Seminar was an incredible experience, with four speakers, Phil, Professor Harold Slusher, Professor Henry Moore, and Professor Custance. We were treated like royalty, taken out for meals in amazing restaurants, shown Niagara Falls, and generally made to feel very special, so unreal and intoxicating, but I shall never forget it. We were so enthused by the whole experience, that Phil and I organised a similar seminar In Birmingham the following year! Over 900 people attended, by ticket only. The speakers were Phil and Dr. Alfred Norris, (Christadelphians), and Professor Geach of Nottingham University and Professor Harold Slusher from Texas. It caused a minor sensation in Christadelphian circles in Britain!

When Vicki was 17 years old, missing her older brother but enjoying young Jamie, who adored her, she became very conscious of the fact that we were concerned because she had not been baptised or made a commitment to Christ, so (as she now explains) she decided to be baptised as a Christadelphian to please us and to be more socially acceptable . Sadly that was her chief motivation and I'm glad we did not realise this at the time, or we should have been heart-broken.

Soon after this, Vicki, having done well in her A levels, was applying to colleges to do a teacher training course. She eventually narrowed her choice to Westhill College in Birmingham, (at that time we still lived in Crawley) and she was immediately accepted at her interview. A slight complication however had come into the equation, the year after Phil and I went to Canada for the Seminar. We returned to stay with the dynamic Farrar family, (Phil had been invited to speak at the Canadian Bible School) and a romantic attachment grew between Vicki and Bill Farrar, so much so, that he came to England to spend Christmas with us! Much correspondence later Vicki went to Canada for six weeks, and it became obvious that Bill was seriously thinking of marriage, even saying he would have a ring with him when he met her off the plane! Such pressure had quite the opposite effect to what Bill wanted, and Vicki was eager to escape from the relationship as soon as possible! With relief, she returned to England to start her course at Westhill College! At that time Westhill had a high proportion of Christian students, with a vibrant Christian Union. Vicki's Christadelphian background and thinking, was challenged as she observed the vitality and joy of the young Christians at Westhill in contrast with her contacts with Christadelphian young people in Birmingham. Vicki courageously blazed the trail for us all as she grappled with doctrines and attitudes that were new to her. Phil and I sometimes gave her a hard time, but what spoke most of all to us was her loving, gentle and Christian behaviour through it all. Eventually we realised that we needed to learn from Vicki, and reassess our beliefs and doctrines. Vicki grew stronger and stronger spiritually, and when she left Westhill, she joined a House Church in London near to her first teaching post at Winchmore Hill, and this is where she met Leslie Wheeldon and her future.

12 MOVING TO BIRMINGHAM

After about five years of applying for jobs, putting off decorating the house and generally living in anticipation of a move, we both started to wonder if God really wanted us to stay in Crawley, and we were fighting against Him! So we changed our attitude, decorated the house, and tried to feel content with staying put. It was as though we stopped struggling and managed to relinquish the whole thing to God.

Within a few weeks, his Head at Ifield School urged Phil, to apply for the job of Headmaster of Thomas Bennett School. (The Thomas Bennett job was highly prestigious, as it was the largest Comprehensive school in the country). He was called for the preliminary interview, which he felt, went well. While waiting for the second interview, a letter came from Birmingham asking Phil to go for an interview at a school that he had not even applied for! Several months before, he had applied for another job in the same group of schools, called the Maypole School. In fact so long had gone by that Phil had destroyed all the information about the school, and the job. So early one morning in September 1973, I waved goodbye to Phil as he set off for Birmingham, minutes before another letter arrived in the post, also from Birmingham, calling him for interview at the Maypole School!

Well to get to the point, after a gruelling interview in front of 18 Governors and Council Representatives, Phil was offered the Job of Headmaster of Kings Heath Grammar Technical School. However before he decided, he was told that he would be also called for interview the following week for the Maypole school job, so he would have to decide whether to accept Kings Heath, or chance it, that he might get the Maypole job. On the principal that God does not play games with us, Phil gladly accepted the Kings Heath job, and he lived to be very grateful that he had not waited for the other, as it turned out, difficult school. The next few months were exciting, very busy, and challenging, particularly trying to sell our house. We bought 89 Arden Road Furnace Green Crawley in 1966 for £6000, now in 1973 the house prices had rocketed and it was worth £17,500! However it was not a seller's market and it took a long time to get a buyer. In fact we were still trying to sell when Phil's new job started at the beginning of January, so for 14 weeks we stayed with two lots of friends in Birmingham, travelling back to Crawley each weekend. As it was a buyer's market, we had plenty of properties to choose from in the King's Heath, Moseley area.

No property seemed right, until one day, Vicki, James and I drove up Elizabeth Road and at the end of the cul-de-sac we saw a For Sale notice. We tentatively knocked the door of No. 64 (because we had no appointment) and Mrs. Davies made us welcome and showed us around. In spite of the fact that the wallpaper was dreary, and the kitchen awful, we had an amazing feeling - this was home! We walked through to the dining room, and drew in our breath as we saw the wonderful garden and woods at the back - in all their Autumn glory! That was it! And when Phil saw the house that same evening, he felt just the same. So we made an offer of £17,500. Mrs. Davies accepted our offer subject to our selling the Crawley house in reasonable time. Then the saga began, the surveyor sent in by the Estate Agent, discovered that the extension that had been described as one of the attractive features of the house was breaking on its back! No planning permission had been obtained to build it, and the Building Society would not give us a mortgage, unless we pulled the extension down before moving in! (Three years after moving in, we rebuilt the extension to our own design).

We then offered Mrs. Davies £3000 less because we would have to rebuild. There was someone else interested in the house, who was prepared to pay £1000 more than us, but she wanted us to have it because we were Christians! To cut a long story much shorter, many nail-biting weeks later, we moved into No.64 Elizabeth Road and so began some of the happiest and yet most challenging years of our lives.

We have never taken for granted the gift that God has given us, and the garden has been a constant source of joy and recreation! It is at times like a wild-life sanctuary, we regularly see foxes and squirrels and numerous wonderful birds; including jays, goldcrests, two types of woodpeckers, nuthatches, tits of all types, and Jim once saw a kingfisher at the nearby pond, we have even twice heard cuckoos. And all this within sight of the centre of Birmingham, two and a half miles away.

We spent some weeks (before moving into Elizabeth Road), going to various Christadelphian Bible Classes to see if we felt at home in any of them. Sadly, we were beginning to despair, when we visited the Christadelphians in Institute Road King's Heath, and we immediately felt comfortable and accepted. Women were even allowed to join in the discussion at Bible class and that was a unique phenomenon in Birmingham. So we joined King's Heath Church and were made welcome by nearly everybody.

Phil found the first few weeks as Head of King's Heath School, very challenging as he felt his way and learned how to deal with criticism and negative attitudes. He developed the ability to detach the criticism from himself, and deal with it objectively and not as a personal attack.

One day I happened to mention to one of the church leaders that I had been involved in running a playgroup in Crawley, and had always longed to start one of my own, run on Christian lines. He proceeded to tell the other church leaders, about this idea, and how good it would be to have one at our church. They then asked me to go to their meeting and explain what my vision was. Thus, I was plunged into organising a playgroup at a church we had only just joined, long before I would have done if left to myself. Maybe it was the way all this happened so quickly that caused keen opposition from a few of the older women, and a confrontation after one Sunday morning service, as they told me they did not want any of my worldly ideas in their church. Even while I was feeling really devastated by their attitude, with tears running down my face, it was as if Jesus was saying "Do you love me enough to face difficulties and opposition for your vision of reaching out to the parents and children who live around this church?" The positive thing was that most of the younger women, and a few older ones, were eager to be involved on a regular basis.

We received permission from the local Social Services to start up a playgroup, we got a few small gifts of money to buy equipment, and as if by chance, someone heard what we were planning and gave us a list of children who were looking for places in a playgroup! We wanted to be as professional as possible, to have a structure to the morning, which included: free play, story time, table activities, and a time to pray and sing. In addition, an opportunity while the children drank their milk, for the mothers to sit and talk about their own lives.

We made it quite clear from the beginning that it was a Christ-centred playgroup, so that parents would be under no illusion about what would be going on. (In the eleven years it was running, only two parents raised any objection to the Christian input!). Some exciting things came out of the playgroup. Once a month we ran a Coffee Morning for the Mums while the children were looked after in the playgroup room. We always had a discussion on some topical subject - (sometimes suggested by the Mums), such as: Activities to do with your children at home, Depression, Abortion, Unemployment etc.

Occasionally, because of some obvious deep need of one or more mothers, it seemed appropriate to pray, and we saw some amazing answers to prayer. Once we prayed for a husband who had lost his job, and within a week, he had found another one. His wife was convinced it was the prayers that did it. Another time, one of the mum's younger sister had been missing from home for several days, and the whole family was sick with worry. Several of us prayed with her - the next morning she came to playgroup with a broad smile on her face. Just after the time we had prayed, her sister had been found! These events were even more thrilling because they caused these non-Christian women to acknowledge and praise God.

I shall never forget one morning when a young and very attractive mother came to playgroup early, one look at her was enough to realise that she was distraught. She asked if she could talk to me in private. Being a trained nurse, she had suspected for some time that she had some strange physical symptoms, and a haunting fear entered her head, that she was developing Multiple Sclerosis! The day before, she had phoned a friend who was a Neurologist, who confirmed her suspicions, from the description she gave him on the phone! She admitted that she was an agnostic, but when I offered to pray she was eager for me to do so. At the end of my short prayer, she said she felt a tremendous sense of peace. Subsequent tests proved that her anxiety had been unfounded, and she lost interest in God! He obviously had not lost interest in her, because some years later I heard that she had become a Christian!

Another vivid memory is of a young Roman Catholic mother, who also came to playgroup early in a very distressed state - she had that morning discovered why her two little daughters had been acting so strangely during the last few months. Their father had been sexually abusing them! She was beside herself with anger and grief, and she never wanted to see him again. As we were praying, and I talked about how Jesus shared her pain and wept with her, it occurred to me to ask her if she had ever really committed her life to Christ. She said no she hadn't, so I suggested that she went home and talk to him, and trust him to deal with her appalling situation. Two days later she came to me and said that her husband had left, (the thing she most wanted for the sake of the girls), and most thrilling of all, she had got on her knees and given her life to Jesus. She was a transformed woman, and the look of peace and joy on her face will always remain with me.

There was one woman, Jean, at King's Heath Church, who worked most closely with me, she came in nearly every day, and we often had lunch together afterwards. One day we were asking ourselves, what other group of people living around our church, could we be reaching out to? We immediately thought of the elderly, so many of whom were confined to their homes for most of the time, often very lonely.

After receiving permission from the church leaders, we started up Coffee Mornings for retired people once a fortnight, and on Christmas Day, we invited them to Christmas dinner and a party. It was wonderful to see their happiness on what could have been such a lonely day. It was not long before the church was buzzing on nearly every day of the week. One particular friend we made from amongst the old people, was Hettie Holder. Through giving her frequent lifts, we got to know her better than the others, and eventually she regularly came to us on Sundays. That went on for about twelve years until she was 101 years old! She had an amazing long-term memory, and she could recite reams of poetry, (of the Victorian Melodrama type), by heart. We missed her a lot when she died in 1995.

In 1974, we had a visit from a dear friend of ours, Lois Finlay. She had booked to spend a week at the Oxford Conference, (a Christadelphian Bible School). As we drove her to Oxford, she kept saying that she wished we were going to the conference as well, so when we were told that they still had some vacancies, and that we could take our nine year old son Jamie, we decided to stay. It was a very enjoyable week, especially because it was our first meeting with Maggie Bates!

At the conference it was the custom to get together in the evenings for discussion of the day's talks, even women were allowed to contribute! One evening we noticed this auburn haired young woman sitting high on a window seat. We were soon drawn to her as she joined in the discussion in an intelligent and lively way. On the following day when some of us climbed the steps to the Jesus College roof to view the 'dreaming spires' of Oxford, I saw Maggie and we got chatting. She asked me if I had read 'The Hiding Place' by Corrie Ten Boon, and when I said no, she said she would send me a copy, as she had found it so inspiring. Little did I know that I had been talking to my future daughter-in-law! Phil and I were so delighted when Laurie and Maggie met each other and started to go out together.

One day early in 1975, a surprise phone call from Alfred Norris, a leading Christadelphian speaker, asking Phil if he would like a trip to Australia to teach at the Mittagong Bible School in place of Alfred, because he could not manage it! Would he ever! It was a wonderful three weeks, seeing all Phil's sisters, visiting Sydney, Melbourne, Adelaide, and Perth, and flying across to New Zealand as well. It was certainly a whirlwind tour, Phil speaking at each place. It was so strange to see people after nearly 20 years and feel almost as though we had never been away!

13 A WEDDING

On our return, Laurie met us at Heathrow, and one of my first questions, which I had been dying to ask was, how's Maggie Bates? Obviously, Laurie was delighted to talk about her, and from then on their relationship grew, until on Dec.27 1975 they were married at Old Trafford Christadelphian Church in Manchester.   The reception was at the Old

Trafford cricket ground Banquet Suite, it was a wonderful meal and such a happy occasion. It was such a joy to us to know that Laurie was marrying such a lovely young woman who loved God and wanted to serve him. We felt confident that they would make a good team.

In 1977, a momentous challenge came into our lives. I think it all began at Hoddeston (a Christadelphian conference centre). Phil and I had been giving an input on family life, and after one very confident talk, a friend of ours came up and said "Don't you ever have any problems in your family?" We replied "No not really". Maybe Satan was listening to our answer and, (as with Job) brought God's attention to it. "Did you hear what those Hawkins' said?"

Shortly after that, the agonising traumas of 1977 started, and went on most of the year. They affected our personal lives, our church life, and our relationship with God. Having gone for months not being able to pray, feeling far from God, and utterly unworthy of His love, one morning, in my bedroom before breakfast, I cried out to the Lord in despair. I longed for him to show me somehow that he still loved me. Tears were streaming down my face as I prayed, and suddenly and unexpectedly, I started speaking in an unknown language! My tears became gushing fountains, and I felt unimaginable joy and bliss welling up in me. All the sludge and evil of my inner being seemed to come out with those tears. I felt clean, forgiven and loved by God, as I'd never felt before. I now understood what it meant to truly repent. I had seen, as in a mirror, what I was capable of, I had confessed my sins, and I knew I had been forgiven. I was 'born again' at last! My Christadelphian upbringing had not helped me to understand that each one of us needs to come to that place of true repentance for the sin that we have done and are capable of. I believe God used my moment of truth, to mould me into someone who could comfort, counsel and encourage hurting people, not from a position of superiority and self-righteousness, but as one forgiven sinner to another. On the morning when this dramatic healing occurred, Vicki happened to be staying with us. I ran into her bedroom to tell her that I had spoken in tongues and had an amazing experience of Jesus' presence. She said she saw at once that something had happened, it just shone out of me! I dreaded going downstairs, in case Phil did not believe me when I told him about my experience. (You see until that day neither of us believed in the gift of tongues!). As soon as Phil saw me, and I told him what had happened, he did believe, and we cried in each other's arms. That evening, Phil was alone in his study praying, when Jesus graciously poured out the same gift on him, so even in that, we were united.

When the news of our experience of the Holy Spirit, broke at the Christadelphian Church in King's Heath, most of the members just did not know how to cope, they were either hostile, suspicious or confused. All sorts of meetings were called to discuss this 'difficult' situation. (Only our friends John and Linda Smith, and Neil Genders, remained loyal and were excited by what was going on). Some even wrote to Christadelphian leaders asking what to do!

In spite of this furore and the numerous rumours which spread around the community about Phil and me, (e.g. that we were having a bad influence on many of the young people), Phil was invited again to speak at Bible Schools in California and New England. He boldly proclaimed the message of Christ living in us by faith. Many Americans came up to him and said "Why haven't we heard these things before, it's so exciting!" It made us very sad that they had been deprived of the living heart of the gospel, and yet were so eager and hungry for it, and so receptive when it was presented to them.

As you can imagine, we were feeling more and more conscious of the fact that we no longer fitted into the Christadelphian mould, and in many ways we wanted to leave, but it was not that simple.

All our friends and relations were committed Christadelphians, and we did not want to hurt them, or imply, by our leaving, that we felt superior to them, or condemned them in any way. However, we knew that Jesus wanted us to follow fearlessly where he led us. In that spirit, we decided to spend one particular week in special prayer for guidance. It was the week before the Oxford conference in 1978. During that week, several interesting and important things happened in addition to the conference itself. There happened to be a significant number of Christadelphian leaders present at the conference, among them was Alfred Norris, who gave a very challenging talk called "Potted History of Israel" in which he mentioned Daniel's prayer where Daniel associated himself with sins of the nation, and their need for repentance. Alfred dropped out the comment - "What can we learn from this?" So in the evening discussion time I asked "In the spirit of Alfred's address, what do we Christadelphians need to repent of?" (On reflection, I suppose it was a cataclysmic question to ask!).   There was a deathly hush, and no one, not even Alfred himself, took up the challenge, in fact, the subject was quickly changed.

The following day as we were walking out of a lecture by another excellent speaker, which we had thoroughly enjoyed, a very influential and vocal sister, turned to us and said "Doesn't that talk make you glad you are Christadelphians?" Surprised by such an odd question we hesitated, and then replied "Well it makes us glad that we have Jesus as our Saviour," at which point she spat out venomously "If you are not of us - get out!" She had such a look of hatred on her face and we both felt devastated. I spent the next hour in our bedroom in tears, and my only sense of peace came when I prayed for her. As the week proceeded, we had three different people say to us -"While you still have a voice in the community, stay, and speak out boldly what God wants you to say. (It was shortly after this that Phil was invited to speak at Bible Schools in the U.S.A.).   So the clear answer to our previous week's prayers was, - stay while you can share the message of the Living Christ to starving people. We were really hoping that the answer was going to be to leave! Another five years were to pass before that hope would be fulfilled.

I now need to go back in order to fill in some of the things that had been happening in Jim's life, (From Jamie to James, and now, by his request, Jim). When we came to Birmingham in 1974, one of our priorities was to find a good school for Jim. We discovered that Moseley C.of E. School had a very good reputation in the area, and after a very pleasant interview with the Headmaster Mr. Sweet, and being most impressed by the atmosphere of the school, it was agreed that he would start the next week. It was a school where they expected and got high academic standards from the students, music had a very high profile, in fact Jim was involved in some outstanding productions. A retired Head of Music, Mr. Walker, from King Edwards Public School, had taken a part time job at Moseley C of E. He was an inspirational figure, and what he managed to get out of those kids was amazing!

Those seemed to be happy years for Jim, and to us they just flashed by. He passed the entrance examination to get into King Edward's Camp Hill School, which was almost within walking distance of our house. Jim soon got involved in sport of various kinds, and he was good at rugby and eventually was in the school team. In some ways Camp Hill was disappointing both academically and musically; as so many bright kids were not stretched to their full potential.

However Jim did extremely well in the Sixth Form, and he took part in some excellent dramatic productions such as 'Salad Days' and 'Hedda Gabler' which they took to the Edinburgh Festival! In his final year he was made Head Boy. Jim was encouraged to apply to go to Oxford University, and after a satisfactory interview, we were all thrilled to hear that he had been offered a place.

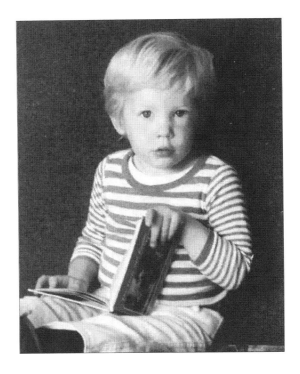

I now want to go back to a wonderful moment in our family, the birth of our first grandson Joseph. It was on October 21st 1977, that the phone rang and Laurie announced with great joy the birth of his son, and that Maggie was alright. We were so excited as we drove to London to see them all. We found it hard to believe that we were actually grandparents! What a joy it has been to have Joseph as a grandson, and see him grow to manhood in what seems such a short time, with all the development of his interesting, thoughtful and Godly personality. We thank God for him every day, and for his lovely parents.

14 LEAVING THE CHRISTADELPHIANS

To return to our journey out of Christadelphia; it was at a Christadelphian Church in Bradford, that the next important event took place. Phil was the preacher for the day and ten minutes into his evening talk a strange thing happened. I was conscious of a voice in my head saying "Phil must give up preaching in the Christadelphians now!" All sorts of thoughts passed through my mind, - 'Is this wishful thinking?' 'Is it really the Lord?' this sort of thing had never happened to me before! So I asked God to show me that this message was from Him. I opened my Bible, and the first words that my eyes lighted on were these - "The Lord God has given me the tongue of those who are taught, that I may know how to sustain with a word him that is weary. Morning by morning he wakens, he wakens my ear to hear as those who are taught. The Lord God has opened my ear, and I was not rebellious, I turned not backward." Isa.50: 4-5.

This passage seemed to convey the thoughts, - stop talking and start listening so that you can begin to comfort hurting people. I still wasn't completely convinced that this was really God speaking, so at the end of the service I turned to my dear friend Pat Young who was sitting next to me, and described what had happened, and asked her if she thought it was God's message. She said she didn't know, but they would be praying for us as we returned to Birmingham. She was convinced that, if it were really a message from the Lord, He would also communicate His mind to Phil in a similar way.

We arrived home and Jim went into the lounge and started playing the piano. Phil and I made ourselves a coffee in the kitchen, then Phil put his cup down on the table and said: "About 10 minutes into my talk this evening, I heard a clear message from God that I am to give up speaking in the Christadelphians." You can imagine the thrill that went up my spine! Neither of us had ever experienced such an undeniable message from God.

Phil was amazed and excited when I told him what had happened to me at the same time during the service! The next day Phil went through his diary which had speaking appointments for the next three years, and cancelled them. He enclosed a letter explaining that he felt God wanted him to take time out to discern God's will for our lives.

Coincidentally with the cessation of Phil's preaching, which had been a highly significant part of his life, my work at King's Heath Church, playgroup, coffee mornings, and work with the elderly, started to dry up. For various reasons, people were no longer available to help, and it eventually became impossible to keep the playgroup going in the Christadelphian Hall. We were able to move to a small Methodist Church around the corner, and with the help of some of the mothers, we kept the Playgroup going, little by little the ties with Christadelphians were being cut. We now realised that the break was inevitable, and would be soon, although we still had not had a clear word from God to leave. My great dread was what my father's reaction would be, frankly I was scared of that. For over two years, Phil and I had been praying that God would help father to understand when the time came.

One evening in the Autumn of 1983, we were sitting in our lounge, when there was a ring on the door bell, and to our surprise a dear old brother from our church standing there, obviously feeling embarrassed and awkward. We invited him in, and he came to the point pretty quickly, i.e. the elders of the church wanted us to resign, reason because we had departed from Christadelphian beliefs. (He had also visited about nine other members of the church, asking for their resignations too). Without any consultation, we all gave the same answer! No we would not resign! Resignation implied that we no longer wanted any fellowship with our brothers and sisters, and that was not true. Many of them were very dear to us, and we no more wanted to cut ourselves from them than from our other Christian friends. When we all reacted in this way, they hurriedly called another meeting and decided to dis-fellowship us all and publish the fact in the Christadelphian Magazine which has a world-wide circulation.

As soon as we saw what was happening, we knew we must visit my father and my stepmother Muriel in Bournemouth - before they read the news in the magazine! So at last, the moment had come when I would have to face my father. Our prayers were answered in a marvellous way. We had hardly been in their house ten minutes, when father said he wanted to go for a walk. I offered to go with him, and I was soon pouring out the whole story of recent events in Birmingham. To my amazement and relief, he was understanding, loving, and supportive, and was most indignant at the way we had been treated! Later when we got back to the house, Phil explained why he had cancelled all his speaking appointments, explaining how God had spoken to us both independently in Bradford. This reminded father of an occasion in Melbourne, when he heard God speak to him, and tell him to visit someone on his way home, with far reaching results. Tears were in his eyes as he remembered, and it seemed to give him a better understanding of our experience in Bradford. Contrary to all expectations, our relationship with father was better after we left the Christadelphians than before.

At about this time, Phil and I decided to go on a Selwyn Hughes Counselling Course at Faremile Court in Surrey. We had heard good reports of it from a friend, and had read Selwyn's book "A Friend in Need" which gave such helpful insights into 'people helping'. First we went to the week-long Foundation Course, followed later by the Advanced Course, (both residential, and in total two full weeks). This was another of those life-changing experiences, which was to lead to our own involvement in counselling work.

Now I want to go back a few months, to December 1982. It was the end of the Christmas term and we were at the farewell dinner given for Phil as he took early retirement from King's Heath School. There were tears in his eyes and heart as he said goodbye to much loved students and members of staff. The eight years at the school had been happy and fulfilling ones, and he was greatly loved by everyone. The assessment of Phil's impact on the school by one member of staff was 'he was a compassionate man' what a lovely and true summing up of Phil's Godly influence on that school. (Phil took early retirement for several reasons, firstly to work alongside Gordon Bailey in Christian Outreach to schools, and also to take advantage of an excellent early retirement package that the Education Dept. was offering at that time).

Jo

1983 was a very challenging year for both of us, and one in which we reached the depths of depression and a sense of loss of identity. So many things happened at once, - the end of Phil's career as a headmaster, excommunication from the Christadelphians, Phil's loss of status as a well-known preacher, all my projects and interests, i.e. playgroup, coffee mornings, old peoples' work, coming to an end. One evening stands out in my mind, we were both kneeling in front of the fire in the lounge praying, and in tears - our world seemed to have collapsed around us. I think we began at last to realise that maybe we had been depending too much on finding our identity in the things that we did, and who we were; headmaster, well known speaker, and wife of same, rather than finding our identity in God. We needed none of these things to be precious to Him. 1983 was a difficult year, but one for which we can now thank God who helped us to get a better values system and greater dependency on Him.

I cannot go on any further without mentioning two amazing miracles of healing. All my adult life I had suffered quite badly at the time of menstruation, and as I reached my late forties it got much worse, the pain almost making me faint at times. I could relate very much to the woman that Jesus healed, when she touched the hem of his garment, because my flow of blood was continuous and prolific. On being examined, it was discovered that I had fibroids on the neck of the womb, to add to the other challenges. All this made staying in other people's houses impossible, because I would have to get up six or seven times a night! (These details are necessary to show you how great was the healing when it came!). Our local GP wrote off to the Women's Hospital for an appointment. A date was set early in the New Year for my operation. From that time, in mid-October, Phil prayed for me every night as we lay in bed. I was dramatically healed! The bleeding ceased, the fibroids were gone, and from that day to this, I have been a new woman! When I explained what had happened to Dr. Kett, he looked a bit nonplussed and embarrassed, however we were able to cancel the appointment at the Women's Hospital!

On the strength of such an experience, when Jim had a really bad problem with his knees, (so bad that he was told to give up all his beloved sport), we prayed for him every evening, putting our hands on his knees. An appointment had also been made for Jim to see a consultant about this well-known and fairly serious condition. However, when the time came, the consultant, accompanied by his group of medical students, was mystified by the fact that the new X-rays showed that nothing was wrong!

Another highly significant event in our lives - was the birth of our second grandson Edward. Eddie seemed to come into the world with a smile on his face! He has always had a fantastic sense of humour. (He and Joseph are in many ways very different, but that very fact has been the basis of an excellent relationship and friendship as brothers).

15 CAMEROON

That same year of 1978 also brought Les Wheeldon into our lives, as our future son-in-law! Les and Vicki met at Winchmore Hill Christian Fellowship, and were drawn to each other almost immediately. Les was studying languages at Oxford University and had been asked to be the interpreter for a conference, in Winchmore Hill, attended by several German churches. Vicki was attracted to his vibrant faith and desire to serve as a missionary in Cameroon, West Africa. The more Vicki got to know him, the more she knew that she wanted to spend her life with this man who was so obviously dedicated to serving God.

Their wedding in August 1980 was a wonderful occasion, it was held in the chapel of Westhill College where Vicki did her teacher training. The minister from their fellowship, Ken Swan, gave an excellent talk, and the whole atmosphere was full of joy. Two of our friends from King's Heath Christadelphians, kindly took care of all the catering, and they put on a superb meal for over a hundred guests, all we had to do was provide the money for the food! The great challenge for Phil and me was the knowledge that our darling daughter Vicki would be living three thousand miles away in Africa.

The separation lasted for seven years, I still marvel at the sense of peace I felt, and the way I was able to release Vicki - contrary to my rather possessive nature. We thank and praise God for the way He blessed the work that Les and Vicki did in Cameroon as they impacted on many lives and established a strong church which was able to continue with the work that had been started by Les and Vicki. They encountered many challenges and dangers in those seven years, some of them life threatening and extremely frightening. (I still have all the letters that Vicki and Les wrote from Cameroon, and maybe one day they will write down their life-story, which would be fascinating!)

In 1985, we spent five weeks in Cameroon to coincide with the birth of Laura, our first granddaughter. As we landed at Douala, Vicki, over a hundred miles away in Nkongsamba, had started labour! Les met us at the airport in the early hours of the morning, it was dark and hot, and so different from the unbelievable cold of Moscow where we had spent two days on the way!! I shall never forget the 120 mile drive to Nkongsamba, it was so totally different from anything we had ever seen before! As soon as there was a glimmer of light from the oncoming dawn, we were aware of people walking along the sides of the road with great loads of things in baskets on their heads, some even balancing oil drums and huge piles of wood. They were walking many miles to market to sell their wares, in order to eke out a living.

Most Cameroonian men and women are tall, stately, and very good-looking. It was from this part of Africa, that many were sold into slavery, chosen for their strength, stamina, and good looks no doubt. At last we arrived at Les and Vicki's home, and you can imagine the joyful reunion with our rather 'less than slender, very soon mother-to-be' Vicki! I must admit that we were rather relieved to find that the primitive dwellings we passed on the road up to their house, were not where we would be living for the next five weeks! It soon became apparent that we would be spending our first night in Cameroon on our own in a strange house, as Les had taken Vicki to the local Mission Hospital.

It was a night to be remembered, with all the amazing insect sounds of the tropics, rising to a crescendo around the house! Next day Les came back to fetch me so that I could be with Vicki as the birth drew near. Words are inadequate to describe the hospital! The people were caring and lovely, but the facilities they tried to work with, were inadequate and primitive. Most meals were prepared by relatives who lit fires on the dried mud outside the hospital huts. No bed linen, and not even basic medical needs such as bandages, were provided, they all had to be brought by the patients. The nursing was done by a relative who slept on the floor by the bed! The toilets were French style holes in the floor, smelly and far from hygienic!

When I arrived, Vicki was in the labour room where she was attended by Cameroonian male nurses, (Les was with her all the time). I spent most of the day, in the two-bed ward where Vicki and the baby would eventually come, no one was in the other bed. I kept making drinks and taking them along to Vicki as her protracted labour continued hour after hour - so much pain - my heart went out to the poor darling. While I was sitting in the ward, I heard strange noises coming from outside, and saw a large group of people leaping and wailing and walking round and round a small building throwing dust in the air. (I later discovered that an 18 year old youth had just died, and these were part of the death ceremonies).

At last, Laura was born, but not without a final agonising trauma for Vicki, who had to have ten stitches without any anaesthetic! She said that it was worse than the entire labour put together! Les went back to the house to fetch Phil, whose lonely vigil was now over, and together we gazed at our newborn gorgeous little granddaughter. To see if she could imitate (as the video had told us) we stuck our tongues out, and sure enough she copied us! What a marvellous achievement at 5 minutes old!

After a couple of days, Vicki was allowed home. It was such a thrill to be involved in this wonderful event in Les and Vicki's life, and to see tiny Laura, developing and exploring her new world. I had taken some nice body lotions and creams, and remember how much pleasure Vicki got when I massaged her back and feet with those sweet smelling lotions. Phil and I found Cameroon quite a challenge, a real culture shock, as different from England as its possible to imagine. Phil did several jobs around the house to help them, and he accompanied Les around Nkongsamba while I stayed with Vicki. Unfortunately after the first couple of weeks, I felt unwell, and that prevented us from exploring the country further than the area fairly near to Nkongsamba. However we did visit the waterfall where "Greystoke Tarzan" was filmed, and on the way there we saw mud brick native dwellings, with their straw roofs, children playing in the mud, and men and women staring with interest, as we passed. Another thrill was seeing a most beautiful butterfly, black, bordered with iridescent blue, with a wing span as great as a small bird! It looked unreal as it took off from a tree trunk near us. We drove by huge coffee plantations with their lovely creamy flowers and heady perfume, no not coffee scent! But reminiscent of tropical flowers like frangipani and magnolia.

Cameroon

A trip into Nkongsamba market was a fascinating experience, and once Vicki was feeling up to it, we went shopping there together several times, the only white women amidst a sea of black faces! They all knew Vicki and were most friendly and interested in us. We watched men embroidering with their much-valued sewing machines, on the African robes of many bright colours. We saw a variety of dead animals hanging up for sale! Hyenas, gorillas, porcupines and snakes, to name but a few! Vicki bought a piece of dead pig with its spiky hair still on it. Stringy tough chickens were also for sale - but our teeth were strong! You did not just buy a bunch of bananas, but an entire branch - and if you happened to leave them in the sun, they went black within a few minutes.

We drove into the English speaking part of Cameroon one day, (Vicki and Les lived in the French zone), and we saw miles of rubber plantations, latex dripping from the incision that had been made in their trunks, into cups, that would be collected later. The British had also left a Golf-Course and Botanical Gardens, in true British fashion!

Towards the end of our five weeks, we all went to mile-six beach (sleeping overnight in a bookshop where the air-con had broken down!). We sat in the shade of the palm trees, nipping into the sea for a quick swim every now and then, to avoid too much exposure to the equatorial sun! We watched a family of monkeys leaping from tree to tree near the beach, and we threw bananas to them, which they caught adeptly and devoured! Even after five weeks in Cameroon, we hardly had any sun-tan as you just don't sun-bathe, it's far too dangerous.

We shall always be glad that we shared this short time in Vicki and Les' life so that we could understand a little more about what that seven years meant to them. We left with so many vivid memories ...

1) The week long Church Crusade, which was held in the Town Hall - loud music - hard hitting challenges - hard seats! - massive response!
2) Vicki crushing huge cockroaches under her heel in the kitchen! And rats eating our bags of sweets that were on the settee, while we slept!
3) The love and friendship of the people in their church.
4) Heat! Rain! Africa!

16 WHAT NEXT?

About this time, Laurie applied for, and got, the job of Deputy-Head of Alleynes School in Stevenage Hertfordshire, so he Maggie and the boys moved from their flat in Bounds Green North London, to an attractive modern house in the old part of Stevenage. Laurie soon settled into his new and challenging responsibilities, and the boys seemed very happy in their Junior School. Maggie decided to work part-time so that she could be around when the boys came home, and her teaching role was with children for whom English was a second language.

What Next?

Soon after returning from Cameroon, we had the pleasure of the company of some young friends, Phil and Gwen Thomas. We were enjoying the sunshine sitting on our patio, and Gwen was talking about her work as a training manager for the Automobile Association. She bemoaned the fact that in addition to all her other responsibilities, she had been asked to design 'Life Skills' programmes for their 17 year old trainees, (compulsory under government funding). Suddenly she turned to Phil and said, "Phil, will you do it?" She then described what would be involved, i.e. Five-day programmes of 'Life-Skills' for groups of about fifteen to twenty, seventeen year olds in various parts of the British Isles. Phil and I discussed it and prayed about it, and we both felt convinced that it was the right thing for him to do.

So in the Autumn of that year, Phil ran his first 'Life Skills' course for the AA at their Headquarters in Nottingham, (with Gwen sitting in). At the end of the week, Gwen said "Phil, I think Jo should join you - it would bring in a unique element to the course to have a married couple relating to the young people." So from then on we worked together, and so began a new and exciting phase in our lives.

When Phil was asked to design these programmes, he could so easily have dipped into the resources that he had been using for years in his school work. But he felt convinced that he needed to have a blank piece of paper and pray that God would guide him to know what He would like the young people to hear. The first impression was -"Give them an experience of Psalm 139!" Obviously opening Bibles was not acceptable in a secular setting, but giving them an 'experience' of that Psalm was possible! "I knew you in your mother's womb!" This approach proved to be an absolute winner, we saw cynical, switched off, young people change before our eyes. We helped them to understand how precious and unique they were as people, how much we valued them, and the wonder of their development from the moment of conception till now.

The five-day programme was designed to bring them to key frontiers of thought, where they would be challenged to think and question and explore the meaning of life. We had some thrilling moments during those three years that we worked for the AA and we now look back on that time, as a vital learning experience to prepare us for the major work of the coming years.

I now want to go back a year, to some important events in Jim's life. The date was December 9 1983. For weeks Jim and the drama group at Camp Hill School, had been rehearsing "Lark Rise to Candleford" - Jim had a leading role, and the final and most important performance was coming up on that day. However in the morning, Jim was in a rugby match, and at about midday, the front door bell rang and Jim's sports master stood supporting Jim, who was in a zombie-like state suffering from concussion! We had to take him immediately into the Accident Hospital, where they said he must stay in for observation. The complicating factor was that, not only was he supposed to be acting in the play at school, clearly now out of the question, but the next morning was to be his baptism at the Church of the Redeemer, and our relatives had travelled to Birmingham to witness it! It was also his 18th birthday!

We tried to explain to the hospital staff next morning, (having rung and discovered - he was now much better) that Jim had to be at his baptism at 10.30am, and please could they release him? No, they said, not until the doctor had examined him! It was nail-biting stuff, but he did make it to the church, looking very pale, and amongst all the drama, our hearts were full of joy that he had made this decision for Jesus, and wanted it to be witnessed by his baptism.

Not long after that Jim, who had been made Head Boy of Camp Hill School, got his 'A' level results, which were extremely good, four straight As, and after a satisfactory interview, he was offered a place at Oxford. Jim's time at Oxford, is of course his story, all we can observe as his parents, is that he enjoyed the unique experience and lived life to the full, revelling in his rowing, and social life, sometimes doing some maths! And coming out of the four years, more mature and a well-rounded person, having survived many temptations and pitfalls, as I'm sure Laurie and Vicki both did when they were at college. So it was straight from Oxford to Radley College, a very attractive public school near Abingdon, to teach maths, and to live in his own flat overlooking lovely golf courses and playing fields.

What Next?

In 1988, we had an exciting trip to Australia during the country's bi-centennial celebrations. We stayed with Lesley, Phil's sister near Sydney, then with Phil's niece Leone in Melbourne, meeting most of the family at parties and barbecues, and having a very enjoyable time. We then fulfilled an ambition that we could not afford to do when we lived in Australia, - to visit Alice Springs, Ayres Rock, and the Great Barrier Reef! All of these experiences exceeded our wildest dreams, particularly snorkelling around the Barrier Reef in perfectly calm water where we could see right to the sea-bed 60 feet below! Words are totally inadequate to describe the beauty of the things we saw and swam amongst!!

While we were staying in Alice Springs, we met up with Lois, Phil's youngest sister, and her husband Don. They lived there in Alice Springs, where they were prospecting for gemstones and gold. They took us gold panning one day, and we still have the minute evidence in a plastic container at home! It was good that Lois made the effort to come and seek us out at our hotel, because, sadly up until then, there had been a strained relationship because of us leaving the Christadelphians. Our six weeks in the land of Phil's birth, will always remain with us as a wonderful memory of happy reunions with family, and exciting adventures.

The following year 1989, Lesley came over to stay with us for three months, and we tried to reciprocate her kindness and hospitality by taking her on a tour of Britain and the continent. We camped in Belgium, Holland, Germany, Switzerland and France, - and covered 3,000 miles! It was a great time and we got to know each other a lot better and had a good deal of fun.

On October 7, 1986, our darling second granddaughter Rebecca was born. Again, Vicki had a difficult time because Becky's was a breech birth, but thankfully both came safely through the ordeal, and Becky lived to add to the joy of our life as grandparents.

Whenever we visited Vicki and Les, the three children always welcomed us so warmly. Laura often wrote loving little notes and put them on our pillows and things like that, which meant so much to us. We love spending time with them as a family as often as we can, especially appreciated after the seven years of being separated from them at the beginning of their marriage.

Leaping forward four years, to another very special event! On June 30 1990, Vicki and Les's son Daniel was born; a gorgeous healthy boy. Laura age 5, and Becky age 3, were thrilled with their baby brother, and helped Vicki look after him. Daniel was a darling boy, with such affection and tremendous potential. All three have their father's big brown eyes! Soon after Daniel was born, Laura had started at their church school in Epsom, where Les was involved in teaching GCSE French and German; as well as his involvement in Pastoral leadership.

A couple of years later, when Becky had also started school, Vicki became involved in running a very lively, and much sort-after, playgroup at the church. Les and Vicki were very happy living in Epsom, and became deeply involved in the Epsom Christian Fellowship, a friendly and caring church, which reaches out in many positive and practical ways to their local community.

On 21 March 1990, my beloved Father died aged 93 - a man who had seen more dramatic changes in the world, than many previous generations. The first car, the first aeroplane, radio, movies, two world wars, and dramatic advances in medicine and science, both for good and evil. The overriding desire in his life was to serve God. He was honest and upright both in business and his personal life. He was a good father, and I have many enduring and happy memories of him and I thank God that he gave me existence.

From 1968, Father cared for mother, day in and day out, for two years, when she was incapable of helping herself. He missed her dreadfully when she died, and we rejoiced when a year later in 1970, he married Muriel Cowlishaw, a life-long friend of our family, who had herself been a widow for about two years. We never cease to thank God for dear Muriel. She gave Father nearly twenty years of companionship and love, and she was a wonderful friend and mother to me. Every moment we spend with her is a source of joy to us. She never grumbled in spite of pain and some ill health, and knowing her enriched our lives.

17 SEARCH FOR A CHURCH

From the time we left the Christadelphians, we were in a sense searching for our identity, and one of the many challenges, was to sort ourselves out doctrinally.   So we tried to empty our minds of a whole lifetime of Christadelphian teaching, and start from scratch to discover Truth, realising that at the end of it, we might come back to some of the beliefs we had started off with - but this time, from personal conviction.   One by one I researched key doctrines in a thrilling voyage of discovery, - Heaven, Hell, the Devil, Judgement, the Trinity, the Holy Spirit, and it was, as if my 'blind eyes' started at last to see, and I was released into accepting the truth of Scripture without the fear of "stepping out of line." Obviously this took place over a long time.   The Lord was so wise, gentle, and patient with us in these challenges!

While this search for identity was happening, we visited the Church of the Redeemer, and it was here that we got to know Gordon and Corrine Bailey better as a couple, (Phil had already met Gordon when he visited King's Heath School.   Gordon made a most valuable contribution to the school life through his Christian input, sharing down-to-earth stories, and Life-Skills with the young people). We see their friendship as a direct answer to prayer at a very lonely time in our life. Gordon and Corrine accepted us just as we were, still Christadelphians, and they listened with understanding and sympathy as we went through the process of leaving and moving on.

Another couple who have played a significant part in our lives from that time were Allen and Heather Cameron, We valued their wise counsel on many occasions. After about two years going spasmodically to The Church of the Redeemer, we started attending the Riverside Fellowship, which lasted for over seven years. We saw it grow from a few people in a house, to a church of over 300. The leaders were Lois and Nick Cuthbert. Nick had a very interesting and dynamic style of speaking, and he attracted many young people from the local colleges and universities. We were happy there, and became quite involved and active as homegroup leaders, running family seminars, and counselling the numerous engaged couples! When the church grew big, the leaders decided to divide into smaller congregations on Sunday mornings, and get together as a large church every Sunday evening. This seemed a wise decision, because it enabled many more people to become involved in church activities, where they were able to use their personal gifts to the full, in a less threatening family-type environment. In addition, sensitive, rejected, and lonely people were catered for in the smaller group, because they were more easily identified!

Then one day it was announced that the small congregations were to be disbanded, and we would now always meet as a large church of over 300. This was a unilateral decision by the two leaders: Lois and Nick, without any consultation even with their leadership team. Many of us were disquieted both by the decision itself, and by the way it was imposed on the church. Phil and I and others, saw that many would be hurt by this decision, and it brought to a focus growing concerns, - too many to be enumerated here. On the final Sunday meeting in smaller congregations, a young woman called Sue Grace, came and gave a wonderful and inspiring talk at our service. (We had known Sue and her husband Fraser vaguely, for a few years, in fact they had attended The Church of the Redeemer when we did, but we had never got to know them really well). We immediately felt drawn to Sue and to her message, and I was moved to write to her, thanking her for her talk, and expressing the desire to get together with herself and Fraser. From this seemingly chance encounter, a deep friendship developed between us, and we started meeting on Sunday mornings. They felt just as we did about what was happening at Riverside. After about three months of meetings, and discussing Bible teaching about: Church; Leadership; the Headship of Christ; the Role of Women, etc; the four of us simultaneously expressed the desire to start a church in the home, where we hoped that lonely, shy, rejected people, would feel welcome and a part of the church family.

The four of us had a meeting with the Cuthberts on May 10 1991, and discussed with them our desire to start a church in the home, which would minister to different needs from that offered by larger churches, (not implying that ours was the only way to worship, but that it was just one of the ways of responding to God's desire for Christians to meet together).

Within a few weeks, we 'launched' Christian Network, which met in our home. Very soon God responded to our prayer! He sent us many rejected, hurting people, including a man serving the last few months of his prison sentence in a clinic for child sex offenders! This man had a dramatic story to tell of one night in prison when he decided to kill himself, he was so desperately unhappy. Before he was able to take the tablets, he fell asleep, and in his sleep he had an encounter with Jesus, and he woke up a changed man. But of course he still had to work through the repercussions of his crime, including his prison sentence. The members of Network unanimously said that they welcomed him to worship with us, and he soon came to look upon Network as his spiritual family.

Amongst others who felt at home with us, were several young men who admitted their homosexual orientation, but who were leading celibate lives as Christians. The fact that they felt loved and accepted led to news spreading amongst their friends, and eventually we had seven homosexuals meeting with us, all of whom had had difficulty in finding a church where they felt welcome. The challenge to us leaders was to show unconditional love and acceptance, without compromising what we believed the Bible was teaching regarding sexual practice, which was part of our teaching right from the start. One of the key features of Network was the participation of all members in the Sunday morning service, full and open discussion was encouraged, and in-depth Bible study was an integral part of each service. We also had a Breaking of Bread each week.

During the first four years, we saw the coming and going of many lovely people. About nine Indian Christians, came to us for a while, in order to get some ideas of how to start their own branch of Christian Network in the Handsworth area of Birmingham. Students joined us, then moved away, but all the while, the core members of the church enjoyed wonderful fellowship, good Bible research. Eating lunch together, and a growing closeness, which developed into lasting relationships.

Four years after Networks' inception, we had a challenge from which the church never recovered. The two most influential homosexuals declared that they had now come to believe that same-sex practice was acceptable, and that they had decided to become practising homosexuals. We the leaders, were desperately disappointed, and saddened by their decision - we also knew that their weaker friends would follow suit - and our hearts broke for them all. An added complication was that they did not believe that a church should have leaders, but each person was responsible for their own actions. A meeting of the church was arranged, and two papers were presented, one researched by Fraser Grace, entitled "New Testament teaching about Church" and the other, by Sue Grace "Sexual Practice - the Biblical View".

These papers were read aloud, and then distributed, so that everyone could read them at their leisure, and we encouraged a Biblical response to the issues raised, none was forthcoming! The upshot was that all the homosexuals left, and a significant number of their sympathisers. Christian Network continued in a small way for another year, and it proved to be a wonderful 'tension free' time of spiritual growth, as we fed on scripture, had communion and ate lunch together. The close finally came, when Sue obtained an important career advancement, which meant them moving to Cambridge. We felt very happy for them, but so sad because we knew how much we would miss them.

So ended a five-year 'experiment' which viewed from some aspects failed - but which those of us who were involved in it from first to last, would say, no! It changed our lives for the better, and the lives of others too.

We continue to pray that the firm but loving stand we took with those young men will bear fruit in their lives for their eternal salvation. (One of them commented as he left, "Thank you for the loving way you have dealt with us, we know that if we realise we have been wrong, you will always have an open door, and will welcome us back").

After the close of Christian Network, Phil and I spent a short time worshipping at home, often with our dear friend Jan Connor. Then one Sunday morning we decided to go to the 11am Choral Eucharist service at

Birmingham Cathedral. It is a very beautiful small cathedral with dazzling stained-glass windows designed by Edward Burne-Jones. We walked in to the strains of J.S.Bach's organ music. We were not used to the Liturgy; however, as we examined the words we came to appreciate more and more the work of Thomas Cranmer who produced the 1552 Prayer Book which is the basis of most of the Liturgy. There were some excellent sermons and a significant amount of Scripture read which helped us to feel 'at home' in this environment.

Over the years we have been attending the Cathedral, we have arrived at the conviction that we are meant to be there, not through any spectacular acts, but through quiet and mostly unobtrusive relationships that we have formed. We have recently become involved in several projects such as becoming part of the Pastoral Care, and the Marriage Preparation Teams. Every Sunday we pray that we may be used to bring comfort, reassurance or help to someone we encounter and this has frequently been our experience, not to mention the times when other people have done the same for us!

There is no perfect Church, and I would dare to suggest, no Christian organisation or individual who has all Truth. Christ alone is the Truth, and as long as we live, Phil and I are in pursuit of the truth that comes only from him.

Earlier I mentioned Jan Connor, she has been, and is, our faithful friend and 'daughter' throughout the years since Christian Network closed. We meet with her almost every Sunday evening for Communion and Bible study and we have all found this fellowship to be of immense value.

18 MILESTONES

On the evening of January 28 1992, Phil came home from a meeting feeling very ill. It was the beginning of a very scary time for us both. Phil's whole body was painful and fevered, and his face muscles were paralysed, he could not even smile. Dr. Baird examined him, and immediately had him admitted to hospital, (he suspected a brain tumour!). Thank God the brain scan proved that it was not a tumour, and they eventually realised that it was a fairly rare post viral syndrome called 'Guillon Barrie'. It was quite a few weeks before Phil felt any better, and even now, years later, he still suffers the after effects with pain in his feet and side. We are so thankful that it was not something worse. He got his smile back.

In 2008 we were greatly saddened when my sister Rosemary went blind as a result of a stroke. The only positive thing was that she came to live in the Christadelphian Care Home in Acocks Green in Birmingham, which is about 12 minutes' drive from us. Olivet is a wonderful Care Home – they treat the residents with empathy and love. Phil and I go to see her every Monday morning and we have a good time together. She knows she can reach us at any time and we can be with her in 12 minutes. We are also able to visit Phil's cousin Bob and his wife Barbara Clare as they have also moved into Olivet recently.

And now – I look back on the Milestones in our ever growing family!

Jo

On July 21 1991, we had the joy of being present at our dear grandson Joseph's baptism. It was a lovely service held in a different church building from usual, because their own, Bunyan Baptist Church Stevenage, was being renovated. We still have a copy of Joseph's declaration of commitment. It was thrilling to hear of his desire to follow Jesus, and to share in Laurie and Maggie's joy. We were particularly touched when Laurie said a few words at the end of the service, to see how deeply moved he was by Joe's decision, one that no parent dare take for granted.

In 1992 Jim, who had been at Radley College for nearly four years, applied for the job of Head of the Maths Department at Forest School, in the Epping Forest area north of London. It was a long shot because of his youth - but it paid off, and he started work there in the September. That meant buying a house in the most expensive city in the country, which stretched his resources to the limits, but it proved to be a very good investment. One comment that was overheard just after his appointment was "I like the boy they have put over the Maths Department!"

1993 brought the joy of Edward's decision to be baptised. Again, we were privileged to be present, this time in their own church building in Stevenage.

Ed, like his brother, is a fine upright young man, who wants to serve God, and that is more precious than anything in the world. The fact that Joe and Ed have made this decision in their youth, will be an anchor for their lives, whatever the future challenges may be.

In the autumn of 1990, when Phil and I were seeking a new direction for our life and work together, we received a phone call from the Reverend Joe Corbett. Out of the blue, he asked if Phil would be prepared to run some counselling courses over at his Christian Outreach Centre in Aston! The amazing thing was that he had only met Phil once about four years previously. While he was praying, and in tears before God that morning, (because of his deep desire to respond to the need for counselling outreach in that desperately troubled area of Birmingham), Phil's name came into his head!

109

After discussing it with me and praying about it, Phil gladly accepted Pastor Corbett's invitation. Phil then spent many hours preparing Foundation and Advanced Counselling Courses. Together we reviewed what we felt were the needs of Christians involved in 'People Helping'. Again Phil wanted us to be involved together, and it has worked so well, each bringing unique aspects to the course, and as a couple being able to relate to other couples in a special way. We were glad we had gone to the trouble of being trained ourselves, at C.W.R. Our programmes were to train people in the skills of counselling. We gained Association of Christian Counselling recognition, and also received academic accreditation with the open College Network via the Bilston Community College, at Level 2 (good G.C.S.E.) and Level 3 ('A' level), which gave an extra edge to what we were doing; covering both the Christian and Secular world of counselling. During those eight years we enjoyed some rich fellowship, and made some wonderful friends.

The most exciting aspect of all this was that Phil and I were working together and we felt that in our 'sixties' we had found the greatest fulfilment of our lives. We believe by God's grace, many lives were touched and 'weary ones sustained' both through our being privileged to help others understand more about the needs of hurting human beings, and in our regular one-to-one counselling. It is so difficult to write that down without sounding arrogant, please forgive me if it does, but we claim nothing of ourselves, we still frequently feel totally inadequate and helpless when faced with so many desperate needs. We cry out for help to the only true Counsellor, he alone knows what is on people's hearts, and he alone can guide what we say to help them. It has been a thrill to be with a wide range of Christians on our courses, and many of them have been prepared to be vulnerable and to share with us some of their challenging and sometimes traumatic experiences. Phil and I learnt so much because of this and through all the varied topics we examined during the programmes. Our aim has always been to encourage lively discussion, and to challenge the 'set' ideas that most of us have, and to be prepared to re-think if necessary.

In the Autumn Term of 1997, Phil and I went back to 'school'! Phil to the University of Central England to do a M.Sc. in Psychology and Counselling! He was offered an unconditional place after a very positive interview, and his 2-year course started just before his 70th birthday!

In 2001, Phil was awarded an MSc with distinction! The only one from his group of students! Not bad for a 70 year old! I was so proud of him as I watched him walk up to receive his degree on the stage of the Birmingham Symphony Hall. From that day to this, he has found what he learned on that course useful when people have come to him for one-to-one counseling and for supervision as counselors.

As mentioned earlier, I started on a teaching course in 1997. It was an introductory course for teaching Adults. The first term was to help each student to decide whether they were cut out to teach! At one point I panicked! I was the oldest one there and I was surrounded by 17 year-olds. On the second week I came out in tears to Phil who was waiting in the car, saying "it's no good I can't do it." Some small thing had upset me and I felt inadequate, but Phil, in his usual loving way said "Yes you can, everything will be alright next week" and he was right, from then on I reveled in the course and some of the 17 year olds became my friends! The introductory term was followed by a further year, at the end of which I was encouraged by my tutor to move on to the University of Central England to do a Certificate in Education which was equivalent to a first degree!

When that was completed (I did well), I was offered a place to start a Master's degree the following week! It took my breath away and I was extremely nervous at the prospect of a Master's course, but at the same time I was thrilled and excited and again with Phil's support and encouragement I launched into this new area of study. In 2003 Phil watched me walk across the stage of the Birmingham Symphony Hall to receive my Master of Arts in Education and Professional Development award! A lifelong longing (To be a qualified teacher) had been fulfilled at the age of 72! I should add that the training I received in those six years greatly enhanced the teaching that I was already doing on our Counseling Training Courses in three areas of Birmingham.

19 FAMILY UPDATES

Fifteen years have passed since I wrote most of this life-story. It is now 2013 and I want to bring you up to date with family news.

JO AND PHIL.

Since last writing my 'Life Story' in 1998, many things have happened, which will be contained in the stories of our three 'children' and their families, and Phil's and my individual stories. I will now try to describe the most important events that have happened to me and Phil as a couple during those years.

In 2005 we had a wonderful 'World Tour' - and full of wonder it was! Our travel agent knew that we wanted to go to Australia and he suggested 'why not do a *circular tour* rather than just there and back'. We thought this was a very good idea and we left him to arrange the itinerary.

On the way out, we visited Singapore, where Vicki and Les were living at the time; in fact we had the joy of Vicki's company for the first five weeks of our tour. The three of us then proceeded to Melbourne – the birthplace of Phil, Vicki and Laurie (who was to join us when we got there – an unexpected extra bonus). We picked up a hire car at Melbourne airport, which Vicki drove all the time, until she had to go back home when we arrived in Sydney.

It was an amazing experience to be with our grown-up children, just the four of us who had left Australia together 49 years previously! We visited key places in the beautiful city of Melbourne that were significant for Laurie and Vicki, (Laurie was nearly five and Vicki was nearly three when we left). A highlight of the time in Melbourne was making contact with Miriam, Phil's oldest sister. We had been told that she would not recognise us because of dementia, but as we walked into her room her face lit up and she said "You're my little brother! It was such a special moment.

We then moved on to Bendigo where Phil and I spent the first four years of our married life and which still had a few hazy memories for Laurie. We took them to see Bendigo High School where 24 year old Phil had his first job. So many warm memories flooded back into our minds, and some challenging times as well.

From there we moved on to Beechworth (famous for being the birthplace of the notorious Ned Kelly) and the home town of our niece Leonie and her husband. We had a great time with them and then we moved on to Albury where we took Laurie to the station to catch his train back to Melbourne. He had only been with us for a week, but what a marvellous week it was!

Next we drove on to Canberra where we spent a happy time with our niece Judith Forbes, and from there, Vicki drove us to Phil's sister Lesley's place at Ulla Dulla. It was so good to be with Lesley, she took us on some lovely walks on the beach close to her house. We talked and talked about fun things and serious things. We never saw her again (or Miriam), they died not long after that, so those memories are very precious.

For the next few weeks we stayed with Julia and Steve Thompson our niece and her husband, and during that time we got to know the amazing city of Sydney very well. In the middle of that time we flew north to Cairns with Vicki and Julia to explore again the Great Barrier Reef and northern Queensland. Snorkelling around and above the Great Barrier Reef is awesome and even that word is inadequate! This time, we travelled much further north than we had in1988.

Then it was back to Sydney and on to New Zealand. We had an unforgettable day at Rotorua, We could hardly believe our eyes as we spent three hours at Te Puia where the mud was boiling and the geyser was blowing many feet into the air. It all seemed like science fiction it was so unreal but so magnificent and breathtaking!

We flew on to Nadi in Fiji. Wonderful hotel, beautiful swimming pool, good food! Then by yacht to two of the coral islands near Nadi (3 hours away). Wonderful snorkelling over coral reefs! Then there was the trip to

Nadi Shangri-La Hotel! Wow what a place! Gorgeous white coral sandy beach, warm water, palm trees, beautiful swimming pool. A hotel for the very rich, but we were able to enjoy it just for the day! It was in stark contrast to the poverty we saw on the way back to our less salubrious hotel!

It took ten hours to fly to Los Angeles with New Zealand Airlines. We experienced November 28th twice as we crossed the international date-line. We stayed for four days in the Hyatt Hotel on Sunset Boulevard, the haunt of film stars past and present! We enjoyed L.A. so much more this time. We went on a four hour tour which took in the Beverley Hills shopping centre, Bloomingdales and Macys where I bought Phil a gaudy tie for his birthday, coming up in two days' time. Next day we went to Universal Studios and then back to our hotel and to pack ready to move on to Denver.

Thursday December 1st and Phil was 78 years old! Very nice hotel all decked out for Christmas and delicious meals! We found out more about the history of this part of America when later that morning we visited the Colorado History Museum.

Next stop Las Vegas and then by shuttle to the Luxor Hotel, a plastic version of the Valley of the Kings! You might well ask what on earth were we doing in 'Sin City'!! Well that is exactly what we asked our Christian Travel agent when we saw it on our itinerary! His excuse was it's the nearest point for the Grand Canyon, which is actually true! Anyway it was a fascinating experience and we didn't gamble a cent, honest!

Sunday December 4th – one of the most wonderful days in our lives! We flew in a very small plane out to the Grand Canyon, passing over the Nevada desert, massive Lake Mead and the famous Hoover Dam. It was absolutely breath-taking as we flew low over the Grand Canyon itself. Words cannot describe how wonderful it is! But the best was yet to come!

We got out of the little plane and into a helicopter and my seat was by the pilot. Under my feet, the floor of the helicopter was transparent! For seven minutes we flew down into the canyon, the pilot then dropped us off by the wide and beautiful River Colorado. A boat was waiting for us and as we sailed along we now saw the canyon towering above us on all sides!

After this, we got back into the helicopter which climbed up an immense height to the top of the canyon. (We were quite sorry to leave the helicopter it had been such a thrilling time!). We were then invited to sit down to a hot dinner, in the open air, at a table overlooking the canyon! I might add, the weather was very cold, so we ate quickly! But nothing could detract from one of the most amazing experiences in our lives. Above all, we felt so thankful to God for his wonderful creation.

It was then back to Denver via Las Vegas and then on to the last leg of our tour, we flew across America to Boston Massachusetts. Our dear friend Debbie Drake was there to meet us at the airport. The Drakes live in a beautiful New England timber house. They made us so welcome and we caught up on each other's family news since we last met. Everywhere looked Christmassy; the snow was so deep that they had to ring for a snow-plough to dig us out!

Milton Drake took Phil and me to visit fascinating 'Orchard House' (the home of Louisa M. Alcott, who wrote 'Little Women'). We then went into the beautiful little town of Concord; it was like a film set with snow and Christmas lights and decorations in the quaint little shops with tiny windows! The date was December 10th Jim's 40th birthday.

Sunday December 11th 2005 – our amazing tour is over. It took us nearly eight hours to fly back to Birmingham. England looked so green. It was wonderful to be home! We were back just in time to celebrate Christmas with our beloved family at Laurie and Maggie's home in Stevenage. We were the only ones with a sun-tan!!

2005 was significant in another way because, just before we went on our world tour, we stopped running our Counselling Training Courses after fifteen years. In that time we had trained several hundred people in the foundations of becoming counsellors, (i.e. up to level 3 OCN). Of course only a fairly small percentage of them went on to develop their skills with further training, but we are sure that both the trainees and Phil and I were changed by doing those courses. To this day we are still happy to see people who need help on a one-one basis, and Phil continues to be Supervisor to several practicing counsellors.

In 2007 Phil was 80 years old. The family and some of our closest friends made it a very special celebration. Laurie and Maggie took the initiative to hire a hall, and beautifully decorate it. Maggie prepared a delicious 3 course meal! There were speeches of love and appreciation of Phil's life, even a message from Vicki and family in Singapore.

I now need to recap our church situation. After being excommunicated from the Christadelphians in 1983 we visited several different churches including The Church of the Redeemer (Baptist) in Edgbaston, where Jim was baptised. (Also Riverside and Anchor; non-conformist churches). We finally joined St. Phillips Anglican Cathedral in 1999. It is now 2013 and we look forward to going to the Cathedral every Sunday! This was not always the case in our past church experiences.

In 2010 and 2011, Phil and I did two courses at the Cathedral during the week. One was a 3D course, (studying the Bible), and the other a Pastoral Care Course. It was enjoyable to have fellowship with other Christians.

However, the main focus of 2011 was our Diamond wedding, and my 80th birthday, both of which we celebrated at the same time. We hired a very attractive village hall at Rowney Green within easy reach, not only of Birmingham, but also close to the motorway for those coming just for the day. It was January 8th (two days after our actual anniversary) and as it was the time of year when illness can be an issue, sadly, seven of the people invited were unable to come because of ill health.

Vicki was in charge of the catering and she, with the help of lots of others, did a marvellous job! Laurie and his sons Joe and Ed, Becky and Jim provided music with singing and dance music! Yes! Phil and I did dance! Jim acted as compare for an adaptation of "Desert Island Discs'. Jim asked us to choose records that had a particular meaning in our lives and why they were so special. Jim did a great job and it went really well.

Our children and grandchildren had clubbed together to buy us the most wonderful 42inch flat screen T.V. It is like having our own small cinema! There were speeches and lots of love from our dear ones; we shall never forget their kindness.

Related in a way to this 60ᵗʰ anniversary was a phone call from BBC (West Midlands) to ask if Phil and I would be willing to come to the studio to be interviewed about our 60 years of marriage and what was the secret of a happy marriage! We gladly accepted their invitation and enjoyed answering their questions. They knew we were Christians and we found it easy to talk about our faith and its central place in our relationship. This was a special Valentine's Day radio broadcast.

At 3.30pm that same day, we went to the Cathedral to be involved in a 'Renewing of Marriage Vows' service. Again Phil and I were picked out to be interviewed because we had been married longer than anyone else! The next day our photos and the interview appeared in the Birmingham Post and Mail, we have never been so famous!

Now updates on Laurie, Maggie and their family:

LAURIE AND MAGGIE.

In 2008 Laurie retired from Deputy Headship at Alleyne School in Stevenage, after working for 23 years under five different Head teachers. He stepped back into the classroom to be an ordinary science teacher and is now Head of Physics at Cardinal Newman Roman Catholic School in Luton. He is happy in this different environment, teaching mainly A level physics and getting involved in the school's music such as his jazz band called 'Cool Cardinals' and a Barber's Shop Quartet.

Laurie has been working with his Religious Education department to give seminars and lectures on the current Science and Religion debate. He has adapted the "Test of Faith" materials from the Faraday Institute for use with 6ᵗʰ formers and has begun to lead sessions in other secondary schools. Several doors are opening for him to take this stimulating course to other schools in London, Manchester and Birmingham.

Maggie retired from teaching in July 2009. However, she is still involved in education, marking exam scripts and invigilating at exams. After her retirement, Maggie was able to visit her mother frequently before she passed away in December 2010.

Laurie and Maggie are members of an Anglican church in the village of Walkern in Hertfordshire. Maggie has been Church Warden since 2007 and Laurie has been a part of the Benefice Ministry team since 2002, which involves preaching and leading services in Walkern, Benington and Ardeley villages in Hertfordshire. They encouraged him to be trained in lay ministry and he was licensed as an Anglican Lay Reader in June 2012. The training for lay ministry has opened doors to further ministry in hospitals, and Laurie has joined the Chaplaincy team at the Lister hospital in Stevenage and QE2 in Welwyn Garden City.

JOSEPH AND CHERYL, TOM AND MILLY.

In 1996, Joe went to London to study medicine at Queen Mary's College/Bart's, where he met Cheryl, who was on the same course, although they actually met at the Dramatic Society. The following year, Cheryl was baptised at the Good Shepherd Mission in Bethnal Green, East London (the church that Daniel now attends).

In 2000, they were married there at a lovely service and in their final year went to northern India, on the border with Nepal, for their overseas "elective" practice.

In 2001, they both graduated and, in 2002, they moved to Leicester, where Cheryl specialised in psychiatry and Joe worked in various hospitals in a range of specialisms.

In 2004, Tom was born on August 28th. By this time, however, Joe had developed serious problems with colitis, first diagnosed in 1996, and in 2005, he underwent surgery.

In 2006, on April 28th, Melissa (Milly) was born.

While working hard as mum, homemaker, etc, Cheryl qualified as a psychiatrist in 2007 and, with some breaks before the children started school, is now practising in a Crisis Response team.

In 2010, Joe qualified as a G.P. and is working in a practice in north Leicester. After some further surgery, his health is, thankfully, stable.

ED AND JENNI AND FREDDIE.

In the year 2000 Jenni was awarded her B.Mus. and the following year Ed was awarded his B.Mus (They met at Kings College London when they were students). Jenni then went on to Homerton College Cambridge for a year to do teacher training. (This was the college that my mother trained at 86 years before!). Following that, Jenni obtained a teaching post at Seaford College Petworth where she joined the music department, until she became pregnant with Freddie. However that is jumping way ahead!

Ed and Jenni were married at Dunstable West St. Baptist Church in August 2003 and Freddie was born on January 28th 2010. The challenge for them as a family was that Freddie was born eight weeks early. His life hung in the balance several times and Ed and Jenni (and the wider family) went through a very anxious time. But now; he is a bright intelligent and adorable three year old!

Ed has been in full-time teaching on four days a week, for 5 years. He has also enjoyed amateur singing for a long time and last year he became a professional singer. At present he is extending his range by doing a course in opera singing. He is a free-lance musician and he plays the trumpet in bands and orchestras. Ed and Jenni attend Arun Community Church in Littlehampton. Ed is in the leadership team and Jenni leads a small group with young women…Exciting news has just been announced that Freddie will soon have a baby brother or sister!

Now Vicki, Les and the Wheeldons:

VICKI AND LES.

When Les and Vicki came back from Cameroon in 1987, they first went to live in Manchester, staying there for three years as church leaders. They were then invited, in 1990, to join the pastoral team of the Epsom Church. For the next sixteen years, their family thrived as they grew up in Epsom, attending the Cornerstone School. Les used his linguistic skills in becoming head of modern languages and Vicki, after a gap of 20 years, went back into teaching at a local primary school, as well as in their Christian school. Then in 2006, Les, Vicki and Daniel went to live in Singapore for two years. Les was invited to become head of Biblical Studies at Marketplace Bible Institute, and to be involved in teaching programs around SE Asia. He also found time to do a Master's degree in Biblical Studies with Trinity Bible School.

Since the children left home, Vicki has been able to travel with Les and be more involved with his ministry of teaching and preaching overseas in many different countries; including – Singapore, Cameroon, Siberia, Baffin Island in the Arctic, China and India. Vicki is also responsible for work every summer, with the young children at the church camp at Rora in Devon.

After returning from Singapore, Vicki and Les are now officially residents in England and have moved back into their house in Epsom.

Les has published two books: 'The Christian's Compass' which is a resource book of biblical beliefs and 'Hearing God's Heart' - a daily devotional.

LAURA.

Laura has also travelled widely; staying one year in Brussels, a year teaching English in Jakarta, Indonesia, then a year in Australia. She experienced a range of different jobs, showing incredible adaptability often rising quickly through the ranks into managerial positions. She is now a project bid manager for Chartwells, working in the Education Section of Compass Group where she is going from strength to strength.

BECKY.

Becky studied German and Russian at the University of Nottingham, traveling to Austria and Russia as part of her degree studies. She obtained a Master's Degree in Soviet Culture. During her time in Nottingham, she met Nick Allsopp at the church they both attended as students. Nick and Becky were married on October 6th 2012. It was a wonderful wedding, full of joy and happiness. They are such a lovely couple, so well suited and above all dedicated Christians. We wish them a fulfilling, blessed and happy life together. Becky is working for Knight Frank as a property consultant where her fluent Russian often comes in useful with visiting investors. Nick works with Ernst and Young and is completing his Chartered Accountancy qualifications. They have a beautiful ground floor flat in Barnes, SE London.

DANIEL

Daniel did the last part of his school education in Singapore, when living there with his parents. He thrived in the atmosphere of the International Community School, enjoying the multi-cultural environment and making close friendships – which was all a life-changing experience for him. These "A level" years gave him a good standard American High School Diploma which then gave him entry to university, to do a Musical Instruments degree at the London Metropolitan University. Here he developed skills in craftsmanship and with his research into rare musical instruments he passed out with a 'first' in his finals. After a year of work experience, Daniel enrolled at Roehampton University to train as a teacher by doing a PGCE in Design Technology. Since then he has got his first teaching job in the Ernest Bevin College, Wandsworth, SE London. Daniel is a deeply committed Christian and takes part wholeheartedly in the activities of the Good Shepherd Mission in Bethnal Green.

JIM, ZOE AND RAPHAELLA.

Jim and Zoe Neeves met at St. Paul's Church in Kensington. We loved Zoe from the start and were so thrilled when she and Jim became engaged in 1998, and were married at the Church of St. Peter and St. Paul in Wadhurst, on July 17th in 1999. Zoe had graduated from the Chelsea College of Art. At that time, Jim was Deputy Head of Chigwell School in Essex. Three years later he was appointed Head of Norwich School where he had a profound influence in the nine years that he was there. Zoe was also deeply involved with activities at Norwich School.

Zoe and Jim's daughter Raphaella Grace was born on September 12th 2004.

In 2010, Jim was appointed Head of Harrow School. It is a school with hundreds of years of history. Many famous people have been educated there, including Sir Winston Churchill; King Hussein of Jordon; Lord Shaftsbury and numerous recent politicians. Jim took up the post in September 2011. We are all thrilled for Jim and we believe he has a great deal to offer the school. Again we are aware that Zoe also has so much to contribute, both to the school and in her constant support of Jim.

Raffy missed her friends in Norwich but she very soon settled into the new school in Harrow. Raffy is gifted and artistic and such a lively and interesting personality. She changed schools again in September 2012, moving to Orley Farm School.

Final Thoughts.

In February 2013, I was 82 years of age! As I write that I can hardly take it in, although there have been quite a few times lately when pain and lack of energy have reminded me that I am indeed over 80 years of age! Even so, I thank God for his blessing of old age, a time for reflection and gratitude for all that God and Jesus have done in our lives, and that the best life is yet to come! Life forever with our wonderful Lord!

In concluding my story I want to add some thoughts about my life which need expressing. In the previous pages, the impression may have been given that my life has been all positive and wonderful! My family have had challenges and have made mistakes as all human beings do, but that is their story. However, as far as my story is concerned, I feel it is important to say that there have been some significant times in my life when I have failed dismally. I am not about to describe these events, or wallow in my sins, but I know that but for the forgiveness of other people and more importantly, the forgiveness and grace of my beloved Lord Jesus – I would never again have found peace or assurance in my Christian life

So I now bring my thoughts and treasured memories to a close - not because my life adventure is over! - but because at the moment I have said enough. I've written these things down for you, my close and beloved family, partly because I thought you might like to know more about the real me! Not just your mother, grandmother, or in-law, and also, that you would be interested in a little detail of your own beginnings and our side of the story. Above all, I hope you will see how God has worked in our lives, gently and quietly guiding and directing (when we were willing!) and occasionally dramatically intervening, may we all continue to follow fearlessly where He leads!

33302474R00077

Made in the USA
Charleston, SC
11 September 2014